FACTS ABOUT
FINLAND

Otava Publishing Company Limited
Helsinki

© Kustannusosakeyhtiö Otava
Otava Publishing Company Ltd., 1991, 1993, 1994, 1996

Published by Otava Publishing Company Ltd.
Uudenmaankatu 8–12, SF-00120 Helsinki, Finland

Text editing by Matti Eskola
Lay-out by Sinikka Lindfors
Translated by Michael Wynne-Ellis

4th edition

Printed in Finland by Otava Printing Works
Keuruu 1996

ISBN 951-1-14471-5

CONTENTS

THE LAND AND THE PEOPLE 5
  Topography 6
  Coasts and archipelagos 6
  Inland waters 6
  Climate 8
  Flora and fauna 8
  Conservation of nature and the environment 11
  Origin of the Finns 11
  Population growth 12
  Settlement 13
A TRAVELLER'S FINLAND 16
  Finnish cuisine 22
Tourist areas 27
  South-west Finland 27
  The lake district 29
  Bothnia 29
  East Finland 31
  Lapland 31
  The rights and duties of tourists 32
  Importance of the tourist industry 32
  Tourist authorities and organisations 33
THE STATE 34
  Constitution and form of government 34
  The President of the Republic 34
  The Council of State and the administration 36
  Political parties 38
  Local government 39
  The judiciary 41
HISTORY 42
  Prehistory 42
  The Swedish period (c. 1200–1809) 42
  The autonomous Grand Duchy of Finland (1809–1917) 45
  Independent Finland (1917 onwards) 49
FOREIGN POLICY 56
  Finland in the integration of Europe 57
  Finland as a member of the European Union 58
  Finland's relations with neighbouring countries 61
  Organisation for security and cooperation in Europe 62
  Global issues 62
SECURITY AND DEFENCE POLICY 64
THE ECONOMY 68
  Foreign trade 70
  Agriculture and forestry 71
  Industry 73
  Construction 76
  Domestic trade 78
  Transport and communications 78
  Banking and insurance 79
  The public sector 82
  Consumption and the standard of living 84
  Balancing the national economy 84
SOCIAL SECURITY 85
  Health insurance 85
  Pension insurance 86
  Unemployment assistance 86
  Accident insurance 87
  Family allowances 87
  Care of the elderly 88
Health care 88
  Health centres 88
  Hospitals 90
  Patients 91
  Environmental health 91
  Housing policy 91
  Labour policy 92
THE CHURCH 94
SCHOOLS AND EDUCATION 99
  Pre-school education 99
  Comprehensive schools 100
  Senior secondary education 102
  Higher education 105
  Research 109
  Adult education 110
CULTURE 113
  Folk traditions and festivals 113
  Traditional handicrafts 117
  Sami culture 118
  Literature 118
  Libraries 125
  Music 126
  Dance 133
  Design 135
  Theatre 137
  Cinema 139
  Architecture 141
  Painting 144
  Sculpture 150
RADIO, TELEVISION AND THE PRESS 153
  Radio and the history of broadcasting 153
  Television 155
  The press 156
SPORT 158
  The most popular sports 158
  Great Finnish victories 158
  The importance of sport in Finland 163
THE FINNISH LIFESTYLE 164
WHO'S WHO IN FINLAND 173
SELECTED BIBLIOGRAPHY 188

Population density map

THE LAND AND THE PEOPLE

With a total area of 338 145 km^2, Finland is the twelfth largest country in Europe. The longest distance from south to north is 1160 km and the greatest width 540 km. Its total frontier is 3600 km in length, 2571 km are land borders; 586 km with Sweden, 716 km with Norway, and 1269 km with Russia. The coastline is about 1100 km long. Approximately 70 % of the land surface is forest, 15 % cultivated land, settlement or roads and 15 % wasteland, such as swamps, artic fells and sand.

The population of Finland in January 1996 was 5 098 754, which makes it one of the smallest countries in Europe. Among the Nordic countries, only Norway and Iceland are smaller. The average population density is 16.7 inhabitants/km^2 of land, which varies from 130 in the industrialised south to between 2 and 3 in the sparsely populated regions of the north.

Finland may be classified as a post-industrial nation, and in 1993 an estimated 8 % of the population derived its livelihood from agriculture, 27 % from industry, and 65 % from services.

Finland is the most northerly country in the world: one quarter of its total area lies north of the Arctic Circle. By air from Finland it is 6600 km to New York, 7800 km to Tokyo and 9600 km to Johannesburg.

TOPOGRAPHY

Part of the Finnish bedrock is among the oldest in the world, and is covered with moraine. The present relief of the country was fashioned during the last Ice Age. The continental glacier gouged the lake basins that run north-west to south-east, and when it ceased it left on its edges the Salpausselkä ridges that run east north-east to west north-west. The fast-flowing currents from the melting glaciers created the numerous ridges, which run in the same direction as the lake basins. The most famous of these ridges or eskers is the lake-surrounded Punkaharju near Savonlinna. Another reminder of the continental glacier is the fact that the land mass is still rising: along the Gulf of Finland the land rises 30 cm every hundred years, and on the Gulf of Bothnia by as much as 90 cm. The land mass thus increases by about 7 km^2 annually.

Most of Finland is low-lying plain. There are lowlands and plains along the Gulf of Bothnia and to a certain extent in the coastal areas along the Gulf of Finland, where the land begins to rise to form mounds and hills broken by lakes and waterways. The average height above sea level is 152 m. The only true highland area is in Enontekiö, Lapland, where Finland's highest points are: Halti (1328 m) and Saana (1029 m).

COASTS AND ARCHIPELAGOS

To the south and west, Finland is bounded by the shallow Baltic Sea, the world's largest basin of brackish water, the Gulf of Finland and the Gulf of Bothnia. The fragmented south-western coastline continues into Saaristomeri, with over 20 000 islands and skerries. As the land is continuously rising, new skerries keep emerging from the sea. To the west of Saaristomeri are the extensive Åland Islands. If an island is classified as a land mass of over 100 m^2 surrounded by water, then there are some 81 000 of them within Finnish territorial waters.

INLAND WATERS

Relative to its size, Finland has more lakes than any other country. There are 187 888 lakes over 5 acres in size, and 22 over 200 km^2 in area, of which 2 are artificial reservoirs. The fourth largest lake in Europe, the 4400 km^2 Lake Saimaa, forms a mosaic of water, rocks, forests and fields in the south-east of the country. Other lakes over 1000 km^2 in size are Päijänne and Inari. The average depth of lakes is 7 m and the deepest ever measured is 95 m. The overall volume of lake water is only slightly more than the average annual rainfall. In many places it is still possible for local residents and summer house owners to drink from the clean, clear lakes. There are over 98 000 islands in the inland waters.

The main watershed is Maanselkä, which divides the waters flowing into the Baltic Sea from those draining into the Arctic

Slamom skiing as well as cross country skiing is very popular in Finland.

Finland's lakes are an indispensable part of the landscape. In summer, Lake Saimaa, the country's largest waterway (4400 km^2), is full of sailing boats. Rafts of logs used to be floated down to the sawmills.

Ocean and the White Sea. As the snow melts in spring, it flows swiftly down the short river courses and may flood, particularly on the plains along the Gulf of Bothnia coast. The longest river is the Kemijoki (552 km).

CLIMATE

The Finnish climate is considerably milder than one might expect from the country's northerly location. The average annual temperature is about 6 degrees Celsius higher than elsewhere in the same latitude. The climate is mitigated by the Baltic Sea, the island waters, but above all by the west winds warmed by the Gulf Stream. In contrast, easterly and southerly winds from the Eurasian continent bring cold spells in winter and heat waves in summer: in southern Finland the average temperature in July can be over 20 degrees Celsius and the highest daytime temperature over 30 degrees.

There are major variations in the seasons. Winter is the longest season, and even in the south the day is short, at worst under six hours. In the north the sunless days of *kaamos* time, when even at midday it is dark, last almost six months, but then in summer there can be as many as 70 nightless days. In the south, a midsummer day is only broken as the sun briefly sinks below the horizon and a milky light fills the sky.

Precipitation is even throughout the year, in winter as snow (some 30–40 % of the total) and in summer as rain. In the south the average annual rainfall is 600 mm/a and in the north 400–500 mm/a. There are about 100 days of rain a year. In midwinter the snow is between 30–40 cm thick in the south and almost 70 cm further north.

FLORA AND FAUNA

Most of Finland lies in the northern coniferous forest zone. There are about 1200 species of vascular plants, 800 mosses and over 1000 lichens. Oak grows in the extreme south and southwest of the country, whereas the Lapp fells belong to the Arctic-Alpine zone. Permafrost only occurs in the most northerly swamplands.

The most important natural form of vegetation is the forest, and the most common trees are pine, spruce and birch. There are abundant swamplands, now mostly drained and forested, but considerable areas have been conserved.

The fauna is typical for a northern coniferous zone. Due to strict protective measures the number of major predatory animals has again increased: the bear, wolf, lynx and wolverine live alongside the European elk, white tailed and Finnish deer, and reindeer, the Saimaa seal alongside the beaver. Over 60 species of mammals have been identified, and the most common in the forests are the squirrel, hare and fox. There are 350 species of birds, most of them migratory, although some like the blackbird

The elk population is considerable, and to keep it in check some 55 000 licenses are issued each year when hunting begins on the 15th October.

The bear, lonely dweller of the wild, north-eastern border areas, wakes in spring from his winter sleep. Bears have increased in numbers and a mature one weighs about 200 kg.

winter in south Finland. The largest birds of prey are the eagle, white-tailed eagle and osprey. There are over 70 species of fish, the most important commercially being the Baltic herring and whitefish. The only poisonous snake in Finland is also the most common;

The white-tailed eagle was once considered an endangered species, but it is again returning to Finland.

Seagulls, once content with the coastal areas, have moved inland and taken over the fields. Another favourite place is Helsinki's market square.

the now protected viper. There are altogether 11 species of reptiles and frogs.

CONSERVATION OF NATURE AND THE ENVIRONMENT

The country's most endangered natural resources are its forests and inland waters, both of which are threatened by acid rain which mostly originates from elsewhere. Due to the sharp contrast in seasons, coniferous forests are extremely susceptible. Those in Lapland in particular are now threatened with destruction unless pollution from Russia can be quickly reduced.

The inland waters of south and central Finland are threatened with eutrophication as a result of industrial, urban and agricultural pollution; due to environmental activists this problem is now under control. Conservation of the soil, groundwater, air and the Baltic Sea are other important fields of conservation. Finland has already approved an environment tax in order to incalcate a more environmentally friendly attitude among industrialists and private individuals.

In order to preserve the country's natural environment in its original state, many conservation areas, national parks and wetlands have been established. Some of these have been reserved for research, but many are open to the public and have signposted walks.

ORIGIN OF THE FINNS

Genetic research has shown that Finnish genes are 65–75 % of European and 25–35 % of Asian origin. Finns in all probability descended from the original settlers that moved into the area after the Ice Age and immigrants from the Baltic region who began arriving about 2000 years ago. Linguistically, Finns, together with the Estonians and Hungarians, belong to the Finno-Ugrian group of languages. Only about 23 million people in the world belong to this group. Colonisation from Sweden began in the first millenium AD, first in the Åland Islands, and later along the coastal regions of the Gulf of Finland and the Gulf of Bothnia.

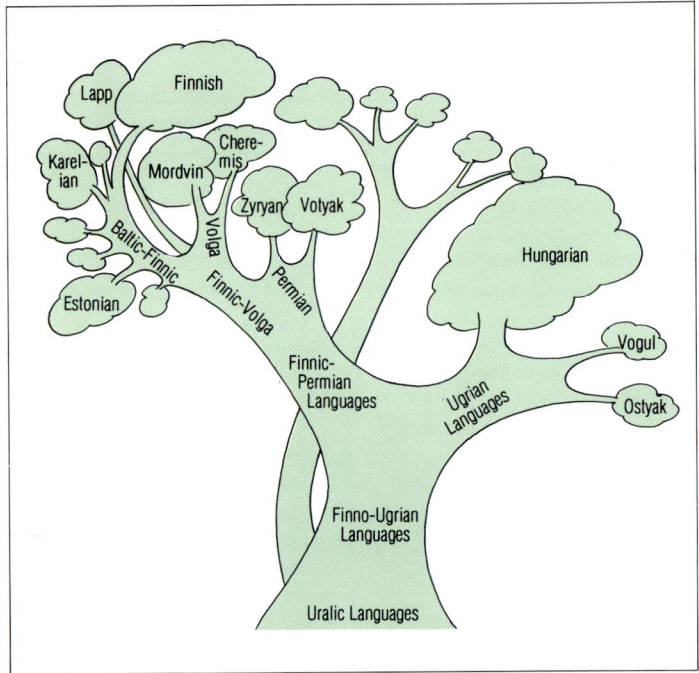

The diagram shows the main Finno-Ugrian languages, spoken by some 23 million people.

The official languages of Finland are Finnish and Swedish, the latter nowadays spoken by only 6 % of the population. Other language minorities are the Sami and Roms. There are about 4400 Sami, 90 % of whom live in Lapland. The Roms, numbering about 5500, live mainly in the south.

POPULATION GROWTH

The first reliable information about the size of the Finnish population dates from the 1750s, when there were slightly less than half a million inhabitants. By 1800 the population was already over 800 000. Population growth in pre-industrial times was very rapid, for by 1870 it had doubled to 1 769 000. Due to improved health conditions and a major decline in the death-rate during the early stages of industrialisation, the population again doubled between 1870 and 1915. After this the birth-rate began to fall slowly, and it was not until after the second world war, at the end of the 1940s, that the population passed the four million mark and finally the 5 million mark in 1991. It has been forecasted, that if the present

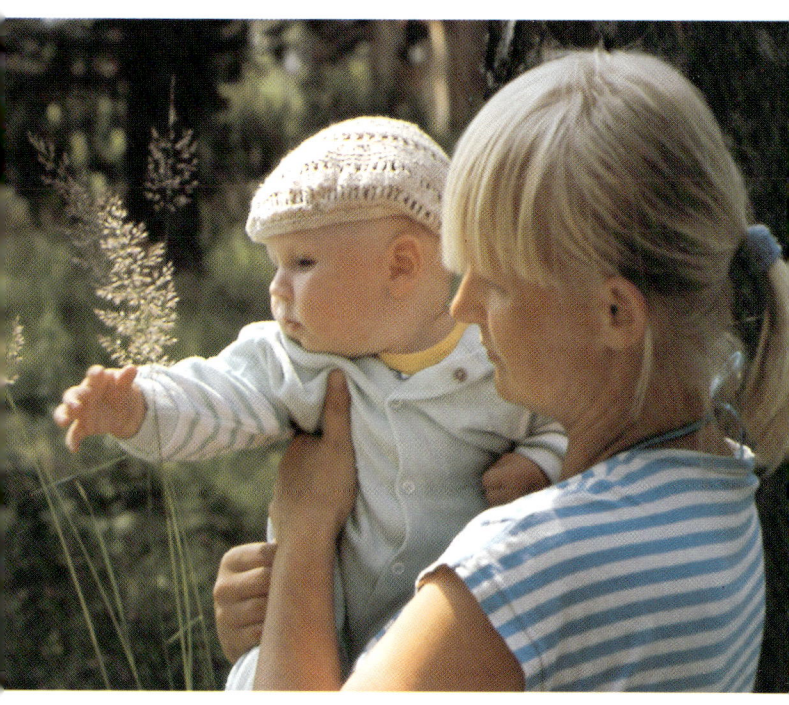

Most Finns have blue or bluish-grey eyes, and fair or brown hair. Z. Topelius, writing in *Suomi 19. vuosisadalla* (Finland in the 19th century), published in 1898, described the Finns as follows: "The common characteristics are: resilience, inner strength, patience, determination . . . a liking for the old and well-known, and a dislike of the new . . . steadfastness in duty, respect for the law, desire for liberty, honesty . . . A Finn is known for his reserve, for his caution. He needs time to relax and get to know people, but when he does, he is a trustworthy friend . . ."

birth-rate continues, there will actually be a fall in population. An important influence on population growth has been emigration. Precise figures are not available, but it is estimated that some 250 000 Finns (400 000 including descendents) have permanently emigrated to Sweden, 280 000 to the United States, 20 000 to Canada and 10 000 to Australia.

The average age expectancy for Finnish women is 80 years, for men only 73 years.

SETTLEMENT

After Iceland and Norway, Finland is the most sparsely inhabited country in Europe. Population density, however, varies considerably. Some 53.5 % of the population lives in the three south-western provinces, occupying only 15 % of the total area of the country. And the population of this area continues to increase rapidly.

This concentration is partly due to the massive process of industrialisation and farm mechanisation that occurred after the second world war. In 1940 some 60 % of the population still derived its livelihood from primary production, yet only 16 % from industry. In the 1950s and 1960s the situation radically changed, and by 1970 the number of those in service trades had risen to almost half, primary production had declined to 20 %, and the share of industry had risen to its present level of about one third. The development of industry and commerce was greatest in the south and southwest, especially in the Greater Helsinki area.

The ten largest towns in Finland (1.1.1996)

Helsinki (Helsingfors)	515 765
Espoo (Esbo)	186 507
Tampere (Tammerfors)	179 251
Vantaa (Vanda)	164 376
Turku (Åbo)	162 370
Oulu (Uleåborg)	106 419
Lahti (Lahtis)	94 706
Kuopio	83 955
Pori (Björneborg)	76 561
Jyväskylä	73 083

(Official Swedish names in brackets)

The Northern and Southern Esplanades, and the park which lies between them, form one of the most charming areas in Helsinki. The park, one of the oldest in the city, extends from the Market Square to the Swedish Theatre, and has statues to three great poets: J.L. Runeberg, Eino Leino and Zacharias Topelius.

A TRAVELLER'S FINLAND

The beauty and pureness of Finland's nature is something remarked on by all visitors to the country. Thousands and thousands of lakes and islands, the archipelago, untouched nature, Lapp fells and rivers, sunlit nightless summers, myriad coloured autumns, "twilight time" in Lapland, snow covered winters, migratory birds returning in spring – all this in a highly industrialised nation whose towns and tourist facilities well equal the standard found elsewhere in Europe. Compared to the countries of Central Europe, Finland remains a clean and peaceful country. The never-ending countryside starts

A glade of spring wood anemones at Ramsholmen, in the Åland Islands.

immediately beyond the towns, varying from ancient areas of settlement to untouched wilderness.

If you fly to Finland, the first thing you notice is the extensive archipelago, a jigsaw puzzle of barren skerries and tree-covered islands, then comes the mainland with its mosaic of lakes and islands, fields and forests. Actually, Finland is one of the most forested countries in the world. Apart from the fact that they are an extremely important source of raw material for Finnish industry, forests play an essential part in every Finn's life. The gods of the ancient Finns dwelled in the forest. It provided the raw materials for works of art and handicraft. Whole towns were built from wood and even if many of them have been destroyed by fire, a few idyllic examples remain. Even nowadays wood is one of the most important building materials used in homes and summer cottages, not to mention the hundreds of thousands of saunas. Outside saunas are built wholly from

Huge ships and ferries now ply the ancient Viking route to the east, carrying over 3.5 million passengers a year. Some two million tourists come to Finland every year, over half of them Scandinavians. The picture shows ferries passing each other in the Åland Sea.

Modern legislation allows summer cottages and saunas to be built by the water's edge in certain districts. For many Finns the dream of a cottage by the sea or a lake is already a reality.

timber, those in apartments and houses are at least panelled in wood. Tasty wild berries and mushrooms are picked in large quantities from the forests, providing such culinary delights as lingonberry, cranberry, or rowanberry jelly with game bird or hare, roast venison or elk. Graceful, lichen-patterned silver birches, darkly festive firs, and stately columns of russet-hued pines reflect the different moods of Finland's changing seasons.

If you arrive by ferry or on your own yacht or motorboat, your first acquaintance will be with the countless thousands of islands that constitute the Åland Islands and Saaristomeri, the world of the archipelago. The barren skerries beyond the Åland Islands, Saaristomeri and Helsinki soon give way to pine-covered isles, through which the "floating hotels" ply their way carrying millions of passengers and their cars between Stockholm and Helsinki each year. In summer the journey is an unforgettable experience as the vessel sails the ancient narrow route between the islands in brilliant daylight or summer twilight. And when a Finn returns home in winter on one of these ferries, he normally visits the steaming-hot sauna in the bows below waterlevel, to listen to the crunch of ice against the walls as the ship ploughs its way through the narrow channel kept open in the solid mass of ice.

If you travel by car, train or bus through the lake district, you will discover a unique landscape of thousands of lakes and islands, where the roads are forced to follow the curving shorelines or cut across the narrow straits.

Typical of the inland waterways of Finland is that they form routes that were the most important means of communication before the coming of railways and roads. Even today you can still travel by passenger vessel between the towns of central Finland.

A great number of Finns spend their free time in summer cottages of which there are more than 400 000, usually by a lake, a river or the sea. Others prefer to travel with a caravan, stopping at well-equipped caravan sites and visiting the many attractions of this extensive country. There are also holiday villages nearby many of the most beautiful areas in the country, with well-furnished cottages or cabins for hire. And for those wishing maximum comfort, a high-standard hotel will be found in even the smallest of towns.

Holiday occupations include fishing, rambling, camping in the forests, sailing, gardening, picking berries and mushrooms, and other things that are close to nature. Summer with its "nightless nights" can be quite warm – over 30 degrees Celsius on really hot days – but Finns also enjoy the rich nature of late summer as hundreds of flowers burst into bloom and the air is full of the songs of birds, or the pure, bright colours of early autumn as it changes into the glowing reds and golds of *ruska*. Swimming in the clean rivers, lakes and pools is a natural part of the warmer season, followed naturally by frequent visits to the sauna. But even in winter many Finns take a dip in the ice or roll in the snow after their sauna. A Finnish summer is best enjoyed by a person who both understands and respects nature.

Many consider winter the best season in Finland because it offers a chance to ski. Skiing in the snow-clad forest or in sunlight over an ice-covered lake is a favourite among most Finns. You can cross-country ski almost everywhere and there are slalom slopes even in the most southerly parts of the country. The best time for cross-country skiing in south and central Finland is in March, when the surface of the snow glitters in the rays of the spring sun. The largest ski centres are in Lapland and central Finland. In Lapland the skiing season lasts well into spring, when the sun shines much longer and you can acquire a suntan. In north Lapland, up in Utsjoki, the snow disappears and the nightless summer begins on almost exactly the same day.

In addition to summer, when the sun never goes down and the daytime temperatures are only two-to-three degrees lower than in south Finland, Lapland offers two other quite special seasons, *ruska* and *kaamos*. During *ruska* nature is aflame with quite unbelievable colours. Many return time and time again to admire the colourful symphony of *ruska*, sometimes heightened against the backcloth of the first snows. During *kaamos*, on the other hand, the sun hardly bothers to rise above the horizon. This twilight lasts for only a few hours but, due to the Northern Lights, the bright starlit sky, moonlight and the blanket of pure snow below, a cloudless night offers an exotic and unparalleled experience, enjoyed even by those who have "seen it all". When the heavens retreat behind the clouds and snowflakes begin to fall, it is time to return inside to the warmth of a log fire and listen to Lapp tales.

In addition to the beauty of its nature and countryside, Finland also offers much of historical interest. Hill forts from pagan times, medieval castles from stone and brick, unique folk-built wooden churches and whole wooden towns have been piously preserved. Coastal fishing villages and idyllic inland settlements associated with traditional iron working, wood processing and glass blowing are well worth a visit. New buildings by Finnish architects of international repute also reflect the special characteristics of this northern nation.

Mid-September is the best time to enjoy the russets of *ruska* at Saariselkä, though both the colours and the time vary from year to year.

Utility glassware has been produced in Finland since the end of the 18th century, but the Belgian, French, German and Swedish glassblowers who came here in the following century taught the art of making crystal and decorative glass. Today Finnish design glass has a world reputation.

In addition to flight connections, there are daily trains to St. Petersburg and Moscow and border crossing points for those travelling by car. There are also trips down the Saimaa Canal to Viipuri. Cultural influences from the neighbouring countries originating from the fact that Finland was first part of Sweden and then of Russia, are particularly apparent in the exciting tensions in Helsinki's townscape.

Sea traffic to Tallinn, the capital of Finland's southern neighbour Estonia, has been particularly brisk.

Political stability and a peaceful way of life, free from the threats of terrorism and violence, have made Finland a popular venue for international conferences, fairs and exhibitions. A flair for organisation and top-level facilities have added to this popularity.

FINNISH CUISINE

Most Finnish restaurants and cafeterias offer typical international food, and many towns have international fast-food chain outlets. The larger towns also offer a number of national and ethnic restaurants; the Russian ones in Helsinki are really something. Funnily enough, the most difficult thing to find is real Finnish cooking, though local dishes are included in many menus.

Finnish cuisine is based on dairy products, potatoes, meat, fish and bread – dark rye bread, for instance, is for many the ultimate personification of Finnishness. Every county, and many districts even, have their own specialities, which are all worth while trying.

Many of these delights are prepared from such freshwater fish as vendace, whitefish, pike-perch, bream, pike and perch, or sea fish like the Baltic herring,

A typical smorgasbord groaning with delicacies.

Finland's most important catch. And salmon from Lapland is something out of this world. Vendace, whitefish and burbot roe is so exquisite that there is never enough left over for export. It should be mixed with onion and smetana, and washed down with Finlandia or Koskenkorva vodka.

Summer's first delight comes in June; tiny, freshly-dug new potatoes boiled in dill and served with butter and raw herring. In July it's time for wild strawberries and cream, the incomparable blueberry pie, and naturally raspberries. Later come the lingonberries and cranberries, and the rarer cloudberries and arctic brambleberries from which excellent liquers are made. The high point of summer is in August, when one of the world's most succulent freshwater delights is served, the crayfish.

In autumn the forests abound with mushrooms, though the tasty morel is already available in spring. There are literally hundreds of edible mushrooms in Finland, but also a few poisonous ones, so be careful and only pick what you recognise. Late autumn restaurants offer such delights as

Gourmets impatiently await the crayfish season, which starts on 21st July. The crayfish are first boiled in water seasoned with salt and dill, then eaten with traditional ceremony in the company of good friends.

Finnish Christmas dinner consists of ham or turkey, vegetable casseroles, herring, salmon and cod.

roast European elk and occasionally roast bear.

The list of provincial foods and dishes is unending. There are all kinds of pies, including the rice or potato-filled *karjalanpiirakka* and curd-filled cheesecakes from Karelia. Another Karelian dish is *karjalanpaisti*, a casserole of different meats and vegetables. One Savo-Karelian delight is *särä*, lamb slowly roasted on a wooden platter. From Savo, too, comes the famous *kalakukko*, rye bread filled with vendace or perch and pork meat, baked slowly in the oven. Ostrobothnian specialities include *leipäjuusto* cheese made from beestings milk and matured over an open fire, and the unleavened *rieska* bread. To quench one's thirst Häme offers a strong, homemade beer called *sahti*. In Tampere they eat a black *mustamakkara* sausage, in the south-west *rosolli*, a root salad with raw herring, and in Lapland *poronkäristys* from reindeer.

Finnish Christmas starts with cod and continues with roast ham and vegetable casseroles, and Easter with roast lamb followed by *mämmi*, a dessert made from rye and malt. Certain national days have special cakes, such as *runebergintorttu* cake on the national poet Runeberg's day, which should be washed down with a "wee tot", *laskiaispulla* bun on Shrove Tuesday, *tippaleipä* cake with *sima* mead on May Day, and the prune turnover *joulutorttu* at Yuletide.

TOURIST AREAS

Finland can be divided into five main tourist areas, each quite different in landscape and culture. They are the south-west, the lake district, Bothnia, east Finland and Lapland.

As Finland's road network and bus system are excellent, all these areas are easily accessible. The rail service extends as far as Rovaniemi in the Arctic Circle and the domestic flight network is very extensive. All transport services offer tourists special season rates, making it possible to travel throughout the country at a reasonable price. The best way to see Finland is by car, and the easiest way to bring it over is by ferry from Sweden, Germany or Poland.

SOUTH-WEST FINLAND

This is an area of ancient historical settlement and the centre of modern economic life. Industry is concentrated around the new capital Helsinki, and the former capital Turku with its fine historical traditions.

Although history is more strongly evident in the inland rural areas, nature is perhaps at its most beautiful on the coast and archipelago. The Åland Islands and Turku archipelago are a yachtsman's paradise.

Large crowds line the banks for the annual university rowing race on the Aura at Turku.

27

The idyllic small towns of the southwest are very popular with tourists. The picture shows the well-preserved wooden houses of Old Rauma.

Between the south-western coast and the Åland Islands lies the Saaristomeri maritime national park.

The largest and most diverse tourist centre is undoubtedly Helsinki, but there are many other interesting and original places in the area that are well worth a visit. Turku with its medieval castle and cathedral, Naantali where a spa has grown up on the site of the monastery of the Order of St. Birgitta, the historic, cathedral town of Porvoo, Hanko for the regatta, Pori for the international jazz festival, Old Rauma with its lovely wooden buildings, and the beautiful port of Mariehamn (Maarianhamina), gateway to the Åland Islands. The coast and the Lohja lake district abound with summer cottages.

The harbour and charming restaurants of Naantali are familiar sights to the thousands of yachtsmen who sail over to visit Finland each year.

THE LAKE DISTRICT
This is the "Heart of Finland", a land of a thousand lakes flowing down the Kokemäenjoki, Kymijoki and Vuoksi rivers to the sea. The main lakes are Saimaa, Päijänne, Vanajavesi and Näsijärvi, and the best way to see them is from one of the ships plying between the towns. The main tourist centre is Tampere, closely followed by Savonlinna, Mikkeli, Lappeenranta, Imatra and the winter sports citadel of Lahti. The most famous natural attraction is the Punkaharju ridge formed during the Ice Age. Another place of interest to visitors is the Orthodox monastery and convent at Heinävesi.

BOTHNIA
The main tourist centres along the Bothnian coast and the low-

For more than a century the landscape around Koli has been the most important tourist attraction of North Karelia. It inspired this painting by Pekka Halonen.

lying farmlands of west Finland are Vaasa, Kalajoki and Oulu. Vaasa and Tornio are important crossing points to Sweden. The Kaustinen Folk Music Festival is the cultural event that most interests travellers in the area.

EAST FINLAND
This sparsely-inhabited area bordering on Russia is a kind of in-between zone between the lake district and Lapland. Its largely untouched nature is studded with clear lakes, streams and forested fells. Karelian and Orthodox cultural traditions are strongest in the southern part, around Joensuu and Ilomantsi, nearby Finland's most famous and pictureseque sight, the Koli Heights above Lake Pielisjärvi. Along the Bard and Border Way the traveller passes through areas associated with the national epic poem *Kalevala* and the battlegrounds of the last war. To the north, in Kainuu and Kuusamo, the landscape begins to look like Lapland, and offers the opportunity for hiking in the wilderness or shooting the rapids. This is an ideal place in winter for skiing and slaloming.

LAPLAND
The very location of Lapland in and north of the Arctic Circle is exotic. Many come here to see the midnight sun or experience *kaamos* in wintertime. Others are attracted by the open fells, autumnal *ruska*, the lure of gold-

Imatrankoski rapids are not only a fantastic sight, but a major producer of hydro-electricity. During the summer the rapids roar for about 20 minutes a day.

panning, angling the ice-cold streams, hiking in the wilderness, cross-country skiing in late winter and early spring, and naturally everything associated with the Lapp way of life and reindeers.

Most travellers pass through Rovaniemi, the gateway to Lapland, as they make their way along the few but highly scenic roads in this region. The largest tourist centre, Saariselkä, is in the Urho Kekkonen National Park. There are several other national parks in Lapland, the most important for visitors are those at Pallas-Ounastunturi and Lemmenjoki.

THE RIGHTS AND DUTIES OF TOURISTS

Camping and caravaning should normally be in the numerous and well-equipped camping sites. Camping out is permitted in certain areas, provided campers observe strict rules of cleanliness and in no way spoil surrounding nature. Hikers should note that nature is untamed, so they should be properly equipped and carry map and compass.

As nature is highly vulnerable, tourists should follow all rules and regulations, and be especially careful not to disturb reindeer. Felling trees, even dead ones, is a punishable offence. Detailed instructions for hikers are available from all tourist centres.

Information concerning passports and visas, work and residence permits, is available from all tourist organisations and

authorities. Most foreign visitors do not require a visa.

IMPORTANCE OF THE TOURIST INDUSTRY

The majority of visitors to Finland come from Scandinavia, Germany, the United States, the United Kingdom and Russia. Tourism accounts for about 3 % of total Finnish exports of goods and services, slightly more than in other highly industrialised countries, but considerably less than in the major tourist nations of southern Europe. The share of tourism in the gnp is about

1 %. The tourist industry gives full-time employment to some 69 000~70 000 people as well as to a large number of seasonal workers.

TOURIST AUTHORITIES AND ORGANISATIONS

There are innumerable offices and organisations throughout Finland catering for tourists. Nationally, the most important is the Ministry of Trade and Industry's Finnish Tourist Board (MEK), which has offices abroad, and the Finnish Tourist Association, which is responsible for publishing tourist guides.

It is easy to become bewitched by Lapland as one skiis over the sparkling snow under a brilliant spring sun.

In the larger centres there are tourist offices, and many districts have their own tourist manager or officer responsible for developing and co-ordinating local tourism.

THE STATE

CONSTITUTION AND FORM OF GOVERNMENT

On the 6.12.1917 Finland declared its independence from Russia, which had become a Soviet Republic on 7.11.1917. For over a century before, Finland had been a Grand Duchy within the Russian Empire, an autonomous state with its own constitution and form of government.

In autumn 1917 the Senate presented Parliament with the proposal that Finland become a sovereign republican state. This was approved on 6.12.1917 and recognised by the Soviet government under V.I. Lenin on 4.1.1918. The constitution of the republic came into force in July 1919 after the form of state had been decided upon. The other important constitutional law is the Parliament Act, enacted in its present form in 1928. Since this time there have been no essential changes to the country's constitution.

The constitution lays down the rules concerning the form and powers of the highest organs of the state, as well as the constitutional rights of its citizens, who are equal before the law. Ultimate power is vested in the people as represented by Parliament. Parliament Act specifies in detail the structure and duties of Parliament and the electoral system. The 200 members of Parliament are elected by direct vote for a period of four years, but the president of the republic has the right to dissolve Parliament on the recommendation of the prime minister before the end of this period and order new elections. The country is divided into 14 electoral districts, from which members are elected to Parliament by the d'Hondt system of proportional representation. The self-governing province of the Åland Islands elects one member. Parliament exercises its legislative authority in conjunction with the president, who has the power to initiate legislation and give his consent to laws. Parliament gives its approval to the government's budget proposal and supervises the work of the government.

THE PRESIDENT OF THE REPUBLIC

According to the constitution, the highest executive power in the country is vested in the president, who is elected for a period of six years at a time. The president is chosen by direct election, with a run-off in case no candidate gets an absolute majority on the first ballot.

The picture shows the colourful garden of Kultaranta, the president's summer residence in Naantali.

The formal powers vested in the president are very extensive. He decides on the presentation of government legislative proposals to Parliament, he gives his consent to laws or exercises his temporary right of veto, issues statutes, calls emergency sittings of Parliament, declares elections, presides over the opening and closing of Parliament, appoints senior civil servants and judges, determines foreign policy and is commander-in-chief of the armed forces. With rare exceptions, the president only exercises his power through the Council of State, over which he presides. The chancellor of justice, who is present at meetings of the Council of State, is responsible for the legality of its decisions. The Council of State is responsible for the decisions of the president.

THE COUNCIL OF STATE AND THE ADMINISTRATION

The president of the republic appoints the prime minister and his ministers, who must be native-born Finns. Ministers and the Council of State must enjoy the confidence of Parliament. Thus although the Council of State is politically responsible to Parliament, the president is not. The president presides over

Party election posters, with Helsinki Cathedral in the background.

those meetings of the Council of State in which the matters dealt with come within his powers – at which time one talks of government – otherwise the council meets under the leadership of the prime minister. The president is not bound to consider the opinions of the prime minister or even the majority of the Council of State, although in practice he almost invariably does so. Although over the decades the exercise of presidential power has varied in accordance with the character of the incumbent, the Finnish political system has remained parliamentary.

There are 12 ministries under the Council of State, each with its own field of responsibility. Due to the division of the tasks of certain ministries between two ministers, the Council of State at present consists of the prime minister and 17 ministers. Matters of major importance are decided at council meetings, minor issues are left to the ministers.

The Council of State and the ministries are responsible only for the major affairs of state. Several ministries have boards under them in which authority is wielded by a collegiate of senior civil servants.

The country is divided into 12 provinces, each with its own government led by a governor appointed by the president. The provincial government is responsible for local administration and other regional tasks. It is, for example, the highest police authority in the area.

Historically, the Åland Islands occupy a special position because, since the Crimean War of 1856, they have been declared an unfortified area in international law. Moreover, they are almost totally Swedish-speaking. Since 1920 they have possessed a large measure of self-government, most recently reaffirmed in 1951. Laws of a constitutional nature may not be changed or repealed without the approval of the 30-member Provincial Parliament chosen at a general election. The islands are administered by a government of seven under the chairmanship of the provincial president, the highest official being the governor.

Central and local government are separated, and the country is divided into 455 municipalities.

POLITICAL PARTIES
Parties are the very foundation of Finnish political life. At the last general election, members of Parliament were elected from ten different party lists. The parties represent different sections of society and opinions, campaign fiercely in local, general and presidential elections, and fill administrative positions from which their representatives exert political power.

Although political life since the end of the war has been characterised by a prolonged struggle between the countryside and the towns, this never prevented the Agrarian Party (nowadays the Centre Party KESK) and the urban-based Social Democratic Party (SDP) from forming coalition governments with the support of other smaller parties. In 1987, however, after decades in opposition, the conservative National Coalition Party (KOK) replaced the Centre Party and formed a government with the SDP. In 1991 the Centre Party formed a goverment with the National Coalition Party as its main partner, and after the 1995 elections the Social Democrats again formed a government with KOK and a number of other smaller parties.

Ever since independence,

Party support in the 1995 parliamentary elections

	% of votes	Seats
Finnish Social Democratic Party (SDP)	28.3	63
Centre Party (KESK)	19.8	44
National Coalition Party (KOK)	17.9	39
League of the Left (Vas.)	11.2	22
Swedish People's Party (SFP/RKP)	5.5	12
Greens (Vihreät)	6.5	9
Finnish Christian League (SKL)	3.0	7
Young Finns (Nuor.)	2.8	2
Finnish Rural Party (SMP)*	1.3	1
Ecological Party (EKO)	0.3	1

* The party has now been dissolved.

Parliament has almost always had a non-socialist majority. As the number of white-collar workers has increased, so has support for the traditional conservative KOK. Support for KESK came mainly from the farmers, but with urban migration the party has now gained a foothold in the towns. Their strongholds, however, are still in north and east. The liberal Swedish People's Party (RKP) mainly draws its voters from the Swedish-speaking minority. The popularist Finnish Rural Party (SMP), which split off from the Agrarian Party in 1959, based itself around the issue of the "forgotten" rural poor. The party disbanded itself after the 1995 elections. The Finnish Christian League (SKL), which like its fellow parties in the rest of Scandinavia draws support from the free church, gained its first seat in 1970. The Greens first entered Parliament in 1983, and the Young Finns and the Ecological party in 1995. The left is represented by the SDP and the League of the Left.

In 1990, the long-divided Finnish Communist Party (SKP) decided to disband itself and reform as the League of the Left, a forum for all dissenting groups of the far left.

LOCAL GOVERNMENT

The constitution grants local government extensive powers. Municipalities are responsible for the administration of their localities independently of the state and for carrying out such duties otherwise prescribed for by law. They are thus responsible for schools, hospitals and health centres, town planning and social welfare. Although they have the right to levy taxes on those living within the area, they also receive assistance from the

Helsinki City Hall houses the offices and chambers of the city board. In front soldiers on their way to the changing of the guard.

central government in proportion to their means. In return the state possesses considerable powers of control over the activities of local authorities, which naturally diminishes their autonomy. Every effort is being made to increase self-government, and a "free-municipality" experiment has been introduced which gives the relevant localities a broad measure of economic independence.

The highest decision-making body in local government is the municipal council, elected by direct, proportional representation, with 17 to 85 members depending on the population of the municipality. This allows quite small groups to be represented. Councils elect their own chairman, and appoint an executive body, the municipal board, for a period of two years at a time. Councils also appoint a number of statutory and voluntary committees to carry out administrative tasks. Because of the proportional system of election, party strengths in councils are also reflected in the committees. The representation of women in these organs is guaranteed by law. Tens of thousands of citizens throughout the country are involved in the work of local government.

The highest local government

officer is the municipal or town manager, who is appointed by the council and is directly responsible to the board.

There are about 400 inter-municipal unions in the country for co-operation and coordination in such fields as hospitals, vocational schools or regional planning.

THE JUDICIARY

The independence of the courts in Finland is guaranteed by the constitution, for it is virtually impossible to remove judges and the judiciary plays a paramount role in their appointment.

There are three levels of courts in civil and criminal cases: general courts of first instance, the Court of Appeal and the Supreme Court. Within the provinces, administrative cases are tried by county administrative courts from which appeal is to the Supreme Administrative Court. Other special courts include the housing, insurance, land rights, water rights and appeals, and market courts and the High Court of Impeachment.

The only link between the judiciary and the political system is that the president appoints the presidents and members of the Supreme Court and Supreme Administrative Court on the basis of the recommendations of the courts. The Supreme Court appoints the judges to the general courts, the other members being appointed by ancient right by the municipal councils. The highest public prosecutor is the Chancellor of Justice, under whom are the provincial police superintendents, sheriffs and municipal public prosecutors. The prison department of the Ministry of Justice is responsible for carrying out prison sentences, its bailiffs enforce judgements in lawsuits and collect fines, tax arrears and debts.

The highest law officer in the state is the chancellor of justice, who is appointed by the president. He participates at meetings of the government and ensures that the authorities observe the laws and fulfil their duties. Parliament chooses an ombudsman, who ensures that courts and civil servants observe the law. Citizens have the right to appeal to either of them if they feel they have suffered injustice at the hands of the authorities.

A new practice has been introduced in several districts whereby a conciliation office endeavours to bring about an agreement out of court between young offenders and their victims, thus preventing the former commencing on a career of recidivism. Community work for offenders is also being introduced.

HISTORY

PREHISTORY

The first people reached Finland shortly after the end of the last Ice Age, when the glaciers had retreated and the land risen above the sea. Genetic research has shown that Finnish genes are 65–75 % of European and 25–35 % of Asian origin. On the basis of language, Finns are assumed to have belonged to the Fenno-Ugrian family. They mainly hunted and fished the coastal areas, and it was not until the beginning of the present era that these people from south of the Gulf of Finland gave this land and nation its name. There is evidence of Stone Age (c. 7500–1500 BC) occupation as far north as the Arctic Circle, though it was mainly concentrated along the coast. During the Bronze Age (c. 1500–500 BC) and Iron Age (c. 500 BC–1150/1300 AD) settlers moved inland, trading and establishing cultural links with both West and East. During the Viking period, there were close contacts with Scandinavia and Russia. When, after their conversion to Christianity, Scandinavians ceased their long-distance raiding, the Finnish and Baltic pagans carried on plundering.

It is believed that the Sampo story in the *Kalevala* is based on the tales handed down by these pagan plunderers.

THE SWEDISH PERIOD (c. 1200–1809)

At the beginning of historical time, Finland was still divided

This 5000-year-old elk head weapon was found in southwest Finland, and many similar ones have been found elsewhere.

The ironmaster's manor of Fagervik (the main building dates from 1773), in the western part of Uusimaa, was one of the early centres of metalworking and market gardening in Finland.

into different and often hostile tribal areas. During the 12th century voyages were even made to Finland from Denmark and Sweden as part of the traditional Road to the East. Up to this time Finland was a political vacuum of interest both to its western neighbour Sweden and the Roman Catholic Church and its eastern neighbour Novgorod (Russia) and the Greek Orthodox Church. The emerging Swedish state tried to establish its old relationship with Finland. The Finns in the southwest and Häme oriented themselves to the West, those in Karelia to the East. Christianity reached western Finland in the middle of the 12th century. Some kind of union was thought to exist between Sweden and Finland. Not until 1216 did the Pope confirm the right of the Swedish king to this area, after which the process of conquest and conversion continued into Häme, Uusimaa and Karelia, where a castle was built at Viipuri in 1293. Under the Treaty of Pähkinäsaari, signed between Sweden and Novgorod in 1323, the most eastern part of Karelia was ceded to Novgorod, so dividing the Karelian tribe between two kingdoms. West and south Finland remained within the western cultural sphere, and part of Karelia came under the influence of Russia and Byzantine. Thus Finland became an integral part of the Swedish state.

Albert Edelfelt's painting The Inauguration of the Royal Academy of Turku in 1640.

Under the influence of Sweden, the Scandinavian legal and social systems took root in Finland. Power was centred in the 13th-century town of Turku, which in time came to be protected by a magnificent castle. Turku was also the episcopal see, and the first Finnish bishop, Maunu I, was appointed in 1291. It was the church that tied Finland to the mainstream of European culture. In 1362 it was noted that Finland had the right to send representatives to the royal elections, and this it did following the establishment of a Diet of the Four Estates in Sweden in the 16th century. The Reformation reached Finland at the same time as elsewhere in Scandinavia, in the first half of the 16th century.

During Sweden's great power period (1617–1721), it controlled the whole of the Baltic region and steadily pushed the eastern border of Finland further and further east. It was Finland, that suffered most from military action in this era, a plight worsened by severe famine in 1696–1697 when almost a third of the population perished from hunger or disease. Sweden also tightened her control over the province during this era, bringing Finnish administration and conditions into conformity with the mother country. Swedes were appointed to the highest offices, the importance of Swedish increased and a process of "Swedification" was carried out to the severe impediment of the fledgling Fennophile movement.

The foundation of Finland's first university, Åbo Academy (nowadays the University of Helsinki), in 1640 did much to advance the academic life of the country, despite the dominance of Swedish.

The end of Sweden as a great power came in the Great Northern War of 1700–1721 with the Russian occupation of Finland in 1714, when the Swedish army was preoccupied on the Continent. This was followed by the period of the Great Wrath, which finished with the Peace of Uusikaupunki in 1721 under which southeast Finland was ceded to Russia. During the Russian War of 1741–1743 the Swedish-Finnish army was defeated and surrended, and Russia again occupied Finland (the Lesser Wrath). Although Russia agreed to withdraw its troops at the Peace of Turku in 1743, the price was further territorial concessions; the eastern border was pushed even further west. Even at this time it was suggested in Finland that the country should separate from Sweden.

Over the following decades the government paid special attention to improving the country's economy and defences. In 1747 work began on Viapori (Sveaborg), an island fortress just off Helsinki. This, the strongest of its kind in the region, a "Gibraltar of the North", was soon followed by a powerful coastal navy. The reign of Gustavus III (1771–1792) saw great improvements in the government and economy of Finland, and many new towns were established. During the 1788–1790 war against Russia, a separist movement began among army officers, which did not, however, receive much support among the populace. Separatism had, however, some effect on Russian behaviour at the end of the next war.

THE AUTONOMOUS GRAND DUCHY OF FINLAND (1809–1917)
In 1807 Napoleon and Alexander I agreed at Tilsit, that Russia would force Sweden to join the continental blockade against Great Britain. When diplomatic pressure failed, Russia attacked Finland, and in the 1808–1809 war defeated its army and

Emanuel Thelning's painting of Alexander I opening the first Finnish Diet in 1809.

occupied the country. Unlike the two previous wars in 1721 and 1743, this time Russia did not withdraw. A peace was signed in 1809 under which Finland was ceded by Sweden to Russia. The importance of Finland to Russia can be understood when considering the defence of St. Petersburg.

The tsar had already decreed that the affairs of Finland were to come under his direct jurisdiction. At the session of the Finnish Diet in Porvoo in 1809, Finns swore their allegiance to the tsar, who in return promised to respect their Evangelical-Lutheran faith, constitutional laws and rights, stating that Finland now belonged to the family of nations.

In being joined to Russia, Finland became an autonomous Grand Duchy, with the tsar its constitutional monarch as represented by a governor-general. The highest organ of government was the Senate, whose members were Finns, and in theory the country had its own Diet of the Four Estates. Thus a separate Finnish state came into being complete with its own institutions.

All major decisions concerning Finland had to be subjected to the tsar, and were presented to him by the Finnish representative at the court of St. Petersburg. A direct contact with the tsar was thus established, so the affairs of the Grand Duchy were not managed via the Russian authorities. The tsar gave every encouragement to the country in order to weaken Swedish influence. The network of canals and roads was improved, Helsinki became the new capital, and work began on providing it with buildings of unprecedented beauty. Most of these still exist, often housing the same state organs.

Finnish national consciousness was strengthened during the period of autonomy: Lönnrot compiled the epic saga *Kalevala*, and the patriotic poetry of Runeberg was hailed with enthusiasm. Snellman, the great statesman and thinker of the period, fought for equality between Finnish and Swedish as the official languages of the nation. Finnish-speaking grammar schools were established. Snellman was most active during the time of Alexander II (1855–1881), when he was a senator and professor at the University of Helsinki.

The national movement gave rise to parties based on language, first the Fennomans in the 1860s and in the following decade the Svecomans. By the end of the century the Finnish side had emerged victorious, helped considerably by the fact that only one in seven of the population spoke Swedish as their mother tongue.

Finland's special status was first questioned by the extremist

The Great Strike in autumn 1905 was Finland's protest against tsarist oppression, and resulted in a new, unicameral parliament elected by proportional representation. Soon after relations between the right and the left so deteriorated that an armed conflict between the Whites and the Reds broke out.

Pan-Slavists during the reign of Alexander III (1881–1894), and later, under the weak rule of Nicholas II (1894–1917), the Russians began to systematically undermine the country's autonomy. The February Manifesto of 1899 so limited the authority of the Finnish Diet that one could talk about a usurpation of power. This led to an unprecedented protest movement, culminating in the collection within ten days of over half a million signatures on a petition to the tsar. This, like another from over a thousand Europeans prominent in cultural life, failed to have any effect. The first period of oppression began. No longer was language the great divider, but the attitude to Russia. The main question was whether to resist all forms of russification or merely defend the position of Finnish. The Finnish Party, particularly the reactionary Old Finns, chose the latter conciliatory path, whereas the Young Finns and the greater part of the organised labour movement opted for opposing all illegal measures on constitutional grounds.

Russia's defeat in the war against Japan in 1905 resulted in a general strike which soon spread to Finland and forced the tsar to liberalise his regime. A radical parliamentary reform was carried out in Finland in 1906, with the introduction of a unicameral parliament, and universal and equal suffrage. The most progressive act was the extension of the franchise to women, the first in Europe to gain full political rights. A new wave of oppression soon began (1908–1914) that went as far as russifying the Senate. Finland's position was reinstated after the February Revolution in Russia in 1917.

INDEPENDENT FINLAND (1917 onwards)

With the outbreak of the First world war, the separatist movement strengthened in Finland, underground activities flourished, and young men left in secret to acquire military training abroad in preparation for an armed struggle.

Following the October Revolution the Senate under

Marshal Carl Gustaf Emil Mannerheim (1867–1951) is one of the most important figures in Finnish history. During the Civil War he was commander of the White forces and in 1918 was appointed head of state. During the Winter and Continuation wars he was again commander-in-chief of the armed forces. It was due to him that Finland stood her ground and peace was achieved, albeit on harsh terms. He was also president for a brief period in 1944. The portrait is by Akseli Gallen-Kallela.

P.E. Svinhufvud declared Finland independent on 6 December 1917 and this was recognised by Soviet Russia on 4 January 1918. However, the radical wing of the Social Democratic Party, the Reds, wished to carry out a Russian-style revolution in Finland. The revolution began in January 1918, with the Reds taking over the whole of south Finland and forcing the Senate to flee to Vaasa. The Civil War, in which the government, the Whites, received help from the Kaiser's Germany and the Reds from Bolshevik Russia, ended in May 1918 with the victory of the White forces under Lt. General Gustaf Mannerheim. This was similarly a war of independence because the Russian troops stationed in Finland were expelled from the country. With the collapse of Germany in November 1918, Finland switched over from an active pro-German policy and turned towards the Allies. The parliamentary system approved of in 1919, a compromise between republican and monarchist interests, gave the President of the Republic a dominant position. He was responsible for foreign policy, was commander-in-chief of the armed forces, and had the right to dismiss parliament.

In spring 1919, largely due to the personal influence of Mannerheim who was at that time head of state, Finnish independence was recognised by Great Britain and the United States. The same year K.J. Stålberg was elected the first president of the Finnish republic.

In 1920 relations with Soviet Russia were normalised when the two nations signed the Peace of Tartu.

In the early 1920s Parliament busied itself legislating for the new republic. Laws were passed concerning freedom of religion, compulsory elementary education, military service, freedom of speech and association, land reform, and prohibition (repealed in 1932). The participation of the Social Democrats in government between 1926–1927 did much to heal the wounds of the Civil War. However, in 1929 the Lapua Movement, modelled on the Italian Fascists, demanded the suppression of Communist activities and forced Parliament to pass the so-called Communist Law in 1930. The Lapua Movement was outlawed in 1932 following an unsuccessful armed putsch. The language question reared its head again during the 1920s, this time the struggle centred around the University of Helsinki where not all subjects were yet taught in Finnish. It was not until the end of the following decade that a final compromise was reached.

Foreign policy was based on collaboration with Poland and the Baltic countries, the fringe

Changes in Finland's eastern frontiers:
1. 1323–1617
2. 1809–1920
3. since 1944

nations who had separated from Russia. From the outset, the cornerstone of its security policy was the League of Nations. When, by 1935, this body had proved itself unable to maintain world peace, Finland issued a declaration that from now on its security would be based on an orientation towards Scandinavia.

The Soviet Union did not accept this and its suspicions of Finnish intentions grew as the European situation worsened. It demanded that Finland cede certain areas in order to strengthen the strategic defence of Leningrad. This the Finnish government did not agree to. In August 1939 the Soviet Union had signed a Non-Aggression Pact with Germany, the secret protocols of which proved incidental to the outbreak of the second world war. At the end of November 1939 the Soviet Union renounced its 1932 Non-Aggression Pact with Finland and commenced hostilities. The Winter War ended with the Peace of Moscow signed the following

In the Winter War Finland fought the Soviet Union alone for three and a half months under exacting conditions, yet survived as an independent nation.

In 1975, the heads of 35 nations signed the final document of the CSCE conference in Helsinki. The same spirit of Helsinki symbolised the gulf crisis summit meeting in autumn 1990. The photo, taken in the yellow room at the President's Palace, shows Mrs Raisa Gorbachev, President Mikhail Gorbachev, Mrs Tellervo Koivisto, President Mauno Koivisto, Mrs Barbara Bush and President George Bush.

March. Though fighting alone under difficult circumstances for three-and-a-half months, Finland had managed to preserve her independence, but at the cost of surrendering the Karelian Isthmus and the outer islands of the Gulf of Finland to the Soviet Union.

Despite the peace treaty, the Soviet Union continued to exert pressure on Finland, whose fears grew when the Baltic states were forcibly incorporated into the USSR in August 1940. Isolated from the West and with Sweden staunchly neutral, Finland turned towards Germany. When the Nazis invaded the Soviet Union in June 1941, Finland followed suit. To have remained outside would probably have led to the occupation of the country by one or other of the belligerents. Thus began the Continuation War, and by autumn 1941 Finnish troops had penetrated deep into east Karelia beyond the old border. Thereafter the front line stabilised until the Russians began their massive counter-offensive in summer 1944, forcing the Finns to sue for peace. Under the terms of the armistice dictated by the Soviets in Moscow in September 1944, Finland's eastern border reverted to that of 1940, Petsamo was ceded, and heavy war reparations imposed. As the German forces in Lapland refused to leave voluntarily, Finland was ordered to drive them out in a bitter war that terminated in spring 1945. The Paris Peace Treaty of 1947 confirmed the terms of the Moscow armistice, which included the leasing of Porkkala, a coastal area near Helsinki, to the Soviet Union, and the heavy burden of war reparations which Finland alone among all nations paid on time.

J.K. Paasikivi succeeded Marshal Mannerheim as president in 1946. His goal was to create a new relationship with the Soviet Union based on peace and trust. In 1947 the Allied Control Commission left Finland, and the following year a Treaty of Friendship, Co-operation and Mutual Assistance was concluded with the USSR. (It was in force until the disintegration of the Soviet Union in 1991.)

Over the following years, Finnish foreign policy stabilised and the opportunities for consolidating the Paasikivi Line improved. Largely due to the effect of reparations, the structure of the economy underwent a radical change. Payment was completed in 1952, the same year as the Olympic Games were held in Helsinki. In 1955 the Soviet Union terminated its 50-year lease on Porkkala, returning the area to Finland. The same year Finland became a member of the United Nations and the Nordic Council. The election of Urho Kekkonen as president in 1956 further strengthened Finland's policy of active neutrality. In 1962 Finland became an associate member of EFTA and in 1973 signed a free-trade agreement with the EEC. Finland joined the European Economic Area (EEA) in 1993 and the European Union in1995 .

Urho Kekkonen resigned in 1981 and the following year Mauno Koivisto was elected president. Finland also hosted the CSCE follow-up summit in 1992 in a totally changed world as the Soviet Union had disintegrated the year before.

In 1994 Martti Ahtisaari was elected president.

The presidents of Finland

K.J. Stålberg	1919–1925
Lauri Kr. Relander	1925–1931
P.E. Svinhufvud	1931–1937
Kyösti Kallio	1937–1940
Risto Ryti	1940–1944
C.G.E. Mannerheim	1944–1946
J.K. Paasikivi	1946–1956
Urho Kekkonen	1956–1981
Mauno Koivisto	1982–1994
Martti Ahtisaari	1994–

FOREIGN POLICY

Sweden's and Finland's common history, and the fact that Swedish is Finland's second official language, have helped forge strong ties with the other Nordic nations. The heads of state frequently visit their neighbouring countries. In the picture, their royal highnesses Carl Gustaf and Silvia of Sweden are with President Martti Ahtisaari and Mrs Eeva Ahtisaari in Stockholm in 1994.

Throughout its history Finland has found itself positioned between the Western and Eastern political and cultural spheres of influence, though culturally and socially mainly on the western side. Geopolitics has, however, limited Finland's freedom of movement as a state. When the country became a member of the European Union (EU) at the beginning of 1995, it could be said it had at long last taken its rightful place in the community of western European nations, that membership became part of Finland's international identity.

The policy of neutrality pursued during the Cold War did not allow Finland to join any western European organisation that could be construed to promote the political values and objectives of the Western allies. One such organisation was the European Economic Community (EEC). Another essential aspect of Finland's western identity, namely full membership of the Council of Europe, also had to wait until the Iron Curtain was raised in 1989.

The leading position of the president in the field of foreign policy was exaggerated during the Cold War. Membership of the EU has increased the responsibility of the prime minister and his government for they now manage Union matters.

FINLAND IN THE INTEGRATION OF EUROPE

During the Cold War, a clear differentiation was made between economic and political objectives in Finland's participation in western European cooperation. Finland could advance further in the economic sphere so long as the balance between western and eastern interests was maintained. Political participation was regulated by its policy of neutrality. In joining the European Union the economic and political dimensions were finally united.

In order to secure its vital economic interests and competitive position in overseas markets, Finland began to participate in European economic integration as far back as the beginning of the 1960s, firstly as an associate member of the European Free Trade Association (EFTA). Once the United Kingdom, Ireland and Denmark had joined the European Community (EC), Finland together with the remaining members of EFTA signed a free trade agreement with the EC in 1973.

Through membership of General Agreement on Tariffs and Trade (GATT) and the Organisation for Economic Cooperation and Development (OECD), Finland worked in close collaboration with the western industrial nations in the fields of international economics and trade. Finland's participation in western integration was balanced by a free trade agreement with the Soviet Union and the socialist countries of eastern Europe and contacts with the Council for Mutual Economic Assistance (CMEA).

The birth of the single market created a need to deepen relations between EFTA and EC countries. This led to negotiations on the establishment of the European Economic Area (EEA) in December 1989. However, before the EEA treaty could officially come into force at the beginning of 1994, most of the EFTA countries joining it had officially applied for full membership of the EU.

According to the Finnish constitution, the president occupies a central position with wide powers in foreign policy. State visits have become increasingly important. The picture is from the visit by President Ahtisaari and Mrs Eeva Ahtisaari to Russia. Their hosts were President Boris Yeltsin and Mrs Yeltsin.

A major change took place in the international situation with the reunification of Germany, the dissolution of the Soviet Union and the disappearance of the ideological divide in Europe. Also the European Community (EC) changed following the Treaty on the European Union signed at Maastricht in 1991, which called for closer and broader forms of cooperation.

In the post-Cold War world, it was no longer necessary from the point of view of political neutrality to remain outside the EU. It would have meant exclusion from the opportunity to influence and decide on matters where the interests and aims of the EFTA and EU countries were broadly similar. The decision was facilitated by the fact that acceptance of the Maastricht Treaty did not require any new security policy solutions upon joining the Union. Finland's accession negotiations began in February 1993 and led to a mutually acceptable result slightly more than a year later. Like the other applicant countries, Finland's negotiated agreement was subjected to a consultative referendum, which gave a clear 57–43 majority in favour of joining.

FINLAND AS A MEMBER OF THE EUROPEAN UNION

Upon becoming a member of the EU, Finland again made a clear differentiation between economic and political participation. The Finnish government has expressed its desire to participate in the third stage of the economic and monetary union (EMU) from the beginning of 1999 as outlined in the Maastricht Treaty and to endeavour to meet the convergence criteria in the appropriate way. Finland also considers there is good reason to intensify integration and to extend qualified majority voting (QMV) in decision making to other areas, such as environmental matters.

In respect to a common foreign and security policy (CFSP), Finland wishes to support inter-govern-mentalism and the independent decision-making authority of member states, especially in defence and other vital issues. Political will and the mutual solidarity of the member states are, in Finland's opinion, more important than organisational structures in making a CFSP more effective. QMV could also be applied in the execution of CFSP measures.

Finland desires that the EU be developed more as an association of independent states rather than along federalist lines. Finland emphasises that the interests of member states should be given equal conside-ration. Openness in the activities of the Union should be increased and it should be brought closer to the everyday needs of its citizens.

As a signatory to the Maastricht Treaty, Finland has approved the long-term goal of a common defence policy which in time may lead to a common defence.

However, Finland does not visualise any development that would compel it to alter its position on military nonalignment or a security policy based on an independent and credible defence. Finns know that the common political obligations arising from membership of the EU promote their own country's security.

In Finland's opinion, NATO and the American military commitment to Europe continue to play a role in the security and stability of the area. In the same way, Finnish and Swedish neutrality contribute towards promoting stability in northern Europe.

Finland considers that it would be realistic and productive within the EU to create a crisis management capability. This could occur by strengthening the operational capabilities of the Western European Union (WEU) and bringing it under the political control of the EU. Upon joining the WEU as an observer, Finland announced its readiness to contribute towards any WEU crisis management initiative (the Petersberg decisions). It has developed a similar readiness to cooperate within the NATO Partnership for Peace programme (PfP).

Finland supports the enlargement of the EU to include the Baltic states and the countries of central and eastern Europe. The goal of membership can be seen to promote democracy, consolidate the rule of law, and strengthen the free-market economies, as these countries will be required to put their relations with neighbouring states in order and solve their national minority questions.

Thus an enlarged EU would bring greater stability to Europe so long as it ensures that it actively develops partnership and cooperative relations with the states remaining outside, such as Russia, thereby strengthening the basis of their reform movements.

The avoidance of new lines of division and the need to preserve stability are Finland's primary considerations in viewing the question of NATO enlargement.

Nordic cooperation, relations with the countries of the former Soviet Union and activities within the OSCE and the United Nations, have all acquired a new dimension following membership of the EU. The same concerns development cooperation. Through a CFSP, Finland has gained adequate participation in dealing

Finnish peacekeeping troops in Namibia before she became independent.

with international issues within the EU, but bilateral relations continue to be a matter of national importance to Finland.

FINLAND'S RELATIONS WITH NEIGHBOURING COUNTRIES

Nordic cooperation is affected by the fact that Norway and Iceland are not members of the EU, although all the Nordic countries belong to the EEA. Conversely, it is just this that has made the parliamentary Nordic Council and the governmental Nordic Council of Ministers such important forums for the discussion of questions concerning European integration. In joining the Schengen agreement on open border crossings, the Nordic members of the EU considered that the Nordic passport union with Norway and Iceland should be retained. Similarly, Nordic cooperation should continue in the traditional cultural and social fields.

A new dimension in Nordic cooperation opened up with contacts to the three Baltic states of Estonia, Latvia and Lithuania following the restoration of their independence. Also bilaterally the Nordic countries have worked to strengthen the foundations of these countries' independence, support their economic and political stability and links to the European cooperation organisations.

Political change in Europe has also opened up opportunities for wider and diversified cooperation within the Baltic Sea region. In respect to Finland's political objectives, it is significant that the membership of the Council of Baltic Sea States unites both the newer and older members of the EU, the countries trying to become members of the Union, and Russia. The Barents Euro-Arctic Council also extends beyond the borders of the Union.

The St. Petersburg area, Karelia and the Kola Peninsular are primary considerations in Finland's bilateral cooperation with Russia. In this, environmental and nuclear security (nuclear power plants) issues occupy a dominant position. Also trade between Finland and Russia, which collapsed with the dissolution of the Soviet Union, has been revitalised and acquired new forms as Russia's economic reform process advances. Numerous joint ventures and projects have been established. Unclear legal and social conditions in Russia slow down or restrict the deepening of cooperation.

Also tourism, especially its economic importance as a result of purchases, has grown. As a producer of transportation and other services, Finland tries to benefit from its position as the gateway between Russia and EU Europe and the rest of the Western world.

Political relations between Finland and Russia are good. Within the EU, Finland works actively to build contacts with Russia and gain support for its reform policies through, for example, promoting technical assistance within the TACIS programme. Although the strong presence of Russian armed forces in the vicinity of the eastern border of the country is not considered problematic, Finland underlines the importance of the Treaty on Conventional Armed Forces in Europe (CFE).

ORGANISATION FOR SECURITY AND COOPERATION IN EUROPE

The Final Act of the Conference on Security and Cooperation in Europe (CSCE, now OSCE) signed in Helsinki in 1975 created the rules of living within a divided Europe. The Charter of Paris, signed at the 1990 summit of the CSCE, proclaimed the shared values of a new era in Europe in which ideological and military divisions had disappeared. Its all-inclusive membership is, in Finland's opinion, the particular advantage of the OSCE in discussing the architecture of European security or when the question concerns monitoring the norms and commitments the members have collectively agreed to.

Emphasis in the OSCE's preventative diplomacy, the peaceful settlement of disputes and, for instance, the monitoring of norms in respect to national minorities and democratic institutions has moved to the newly independent states resulting from the break-up of the Soviet Union and the work of political reconstruction in the former Yugoslavia. Here the OSCE receives the full support of Finland as indeed the whole of the EU.

GLOBAL ISSUES

The United Nations Organisation, and the special conferences it arranges, continues to play a central role in the handling of global issues. Finland considers that the UN Security Council (or the OSCE) should continue to function as the political mandator of international peacekeeping and crisis management operations in which Finland could participate.

Due to changes in the nature

and requirements of peacekeeping operations, Finland could accept that operative leadership be given to some other organisation, like NATO in the case of the IFOR force. This, as well as the adaptation of rules concerning the use of armed force to meet changing requirements, have enabled Finland to participate in the IFOR operation in Bosnia-Herzegovina. In this way Finland may, even under changing conditions, continue its traditionally active participation in peacekeeping operations, though Finnish law does not permit participation in peace enforcement.

Finland, which has twice been a member of the UN Security Council (1969–70 and 1989-90), considers it important to maintain the effectiveness of the Council whilst at the same time bringing its membership into line with the realities of the international balance of power. Likewise Finland supports the reform of UN institutions and measures to improve their efficiency. In addition, Finland hopes that all member states will meet their financial obligations to the United Nations.

In the field of weapons control policy, Finland is a member of numerous control systems which aim at preventing the spread of nuclear weapons, and the technology for the production of nuclear weapons and missiles. Similarly Finland has developed its capability to contribute towards monitoring agreements banning chemical weapons and underground nuclear tests.

Due to cutbacks in public spending in the 1990s, Finland has had to reduce its contribution to development cooperation work from over 0.7 % of gdp to nearer 0.3 %. These reductions have affected both bilateral and international development projects. Finland has committed itself politically and publicly to the goal of regaining the earlier level by the first decade of the 21st century. Through its contribution to the EU, Finland also helps to finance European Commission development cooperation projects and the EU has become a new channel for multilateral development cooperation.

The goal of Finnish development cooperation work is to develop the human resources and independent capability of the receiving countries. Both bilaterally and multilaterally within the EU and other bodies, the political objectives of Finnish development cooperation are to promote equality, democracy and human rights, and demand that these, as well as environmental considerations, are respected. These then are the basic tenets of Finnish foreign policy.

SECURITY AND DEFENCE POLICY

With the end to the Cold War, the military situation in Europe changed so that the threat of a major war diminished. The new politico-security problems that have arisen since then concern conflicts within states or of limited territorial nature, nationality disputes, and others due to political instability.

The guidelines for Finnish security policy were set out in a report of the Council of State given to Parliament in June 1995 entitled "Security in a Changing World". The task of Finnish security policy is to preserve the country's independence, to safeguard the basic values of the society and to guarantee Finland's political capability. Security policy should serve Finland as a civic society, an independent state and a member of the international community. It should provide Finland with opportunities for influencing international decisions affecting the country and protecting it from risks and threats to its security.

Finland pursues a policy of military nonalignment. Finland's defence solution is based on territorial defence and a large reserve army founded on universal military service. Finland's credible independent

A soldier from the Lapp Brigade on winter manoeuvres.

Finland has ordered a fleet of new Hornet fighter planes.

defence capability is the best way to guarantee that Finnish territory will not become the object of military speculation, or that a war will result from the threat of military force in even minor crises.

The president of the republic is the supreme commander of the defence forces. The Defence Council is the highest consultative and planning body on defence matters. Its members are the ministers concerned with defence and the Chief of Defence and the Chief of Defence Staff. As a part of the Council of State, the Ministry of Defence is responsible for national defence policy and security, as well as international cooperation in defence questions. The Chief of the Defence forces leads the defence forces which are responsible for securing the territorial integrity of the country in practice, and the defence of the nation and its military preparedness in general. Administratively, the defence forces are under the Ministry of Defence. In respect to military orders, the Chief of the Defence forces is directly responsible to the president.

Territorial defence is laid down in the 1974 Defence Act. In addition to military defence, this also includes safeguarding the economy, civil defence, and measures relating to defence information, social welfare, health care, communications, civil order and security. In accordance with the 1991 State of Readiness Act, the defence of the nation is shared between several different administrative sectors.

The country is divided into three commands and 12 military provinces, thus ensuring that the whole territory is defended. The most important tasks of the defence forces are the surveillance of the nation's land, sea and air spaces, securing territorial integrity and, if necessary, the defence of the country. Responsibility for guarding the nation's borders rests with the Border Guard Service under the Ministry of the Interior.

According to Finnish law, all male citizens between the ages of 17 and 60 are under an obligation to carry out military service. Military service lasts 240, 285 or 330 days. Each year about 85 % of those called up do their military service. The wartime strength of the Finnish defence force is about 500 000 men. An essential part of military service is attendance on reserve military training. In accordance with a law passed in 1995, it is now possible for women to volunteer for military service.

In recent years Finland has spent about 1.5 % of its gdp on military defence, which is about 5 % of the annual budget. An essential part of the defence force's capability is its physical preparedness, and about one-third of defence expenditure is spent on materiel.

The goal of defence policy is to ensure the resources and other prerequisites for the independent military defence of the nation. In addition to national defence policy, international cooperation has become increasingly important. Finland's membership of the European Union increases the security of the nation and offers new opportunities for influencing its security environment. Finland is part of NATO's Partnership for Peace programme (PfP) and is an observer in the Western European Union (WEU). Through cooperation, the preconditions for international crisis management are created, as well as the possibility of influencing European security structures in the national interest. For decades now Finland has participated in UN peacekeeping operations. Finland considers that such operations will continue to be important in the future, as the need for crisis management has grown within the international community.

THE ECONOMY

Finland after the second world war could still be considered a semi-industrialised nation as the majority of the population was still engaged in agriculture and forestry. As late as 1950 46 % of the labour force worked in primary production, and some 27 % each in industry and services. Incomes were relatively low, rationing was still in force, and exports were unbalanced. One result of the heavy bill for war reparations to the Soviet Union was that Finland was forced to industrialise quickly.

From 1950 to 1974 the real growth in gdp was rapid, averaging 5 % per annum, so already in the 1970s Finland could be considered a highly developed postindustrial country. Since 1975 the growth in gdp has slowed down somewhat, although in the boom years of the 1980s it again increased to almost 6 per cent.

This ceased as Finland entered a recession at the beginning of the 1990s, the reasons for which were the excessive overheating of the economy towards the end of the preceding decade, central and local government and corporate indebtedness, immoderate expansion during the 1970s and 1980s in the public sector, a growing balance of payments' deficit, and the simultaneous collapse of trade with the Soviet Union. The economy went into decline at the beginning of the 1990s, unemployment increased and the Finn markka was removed from its ties to the ECU within the EMS and allowed to float, thereby effectively devaluing it by some 25 per cent. However, by 1995 the markka had regained its previous value.

Calculated at market prices, per capita gdp in Finland in 1990 was one of the highest in the world. As a result of rapid industrialisation, the standard of living had by international criteria reached a high level. However, because of high costs largely due to climatic conditions, the purchasing power of Finnish incomes is somewhat lower, yet still above average for Europe.

The population has rapidly urbanised, and the structure of both industry and foreign trade radically changed. The main features of Finnish economic life today are the internationalisation of its corporations and the production and utilisation of advanced technology. Nowadays, only 8 % of the labour force is engaged in primary production and 30 % in industry, whereas services account for 60 % per cent. Although about 44 % of the labour force has only received a basic education, a similar percentage has acquired vocational or professional training and some 12 % a university education.

Even during the worst period of the recession the shipbuilding industry's order books were full. The picture shows the luxury liners M/S Sensation and M/S Fascination under construction at Kværner Masa-Yards in Helsinki.

Countless lakes and a long coastline not only lure Finns to the water, but have given them an incomparable skill in boat building. Skimming over the waters in a Swan boat is a sure way of forgetting everyday worries.

Finnish economic life is based on private ownership and free enterprise. In certain sectors, however, the state has a monopoly. For example, ALKO has had the sole right to sell wines and spirits, and the railways (Valtionrautatiet), air traffic (Finnair), oil refining (Neste) and electricity (Imatran Voima) have also occupied monopoly positions, but this system is rapidly changing.

FOREIGN TRADE

Due to the limited size of the domestic market, foreign trade is of vital importance to the Finnish economy.

In the first half of the present century exports relied heavily on the forest industry, particularly the products of the wood and paper industries. During the fifties, the metal and engineering industries began massive exports to the Soviet Union. With the growing integration of trade in Western Europe, Finland, in order to safeguard its export markets, joined EFTA under the FINEFTA Agreement of 1961. Along with other neutral nations, Finland signed a special free-trade agreement with the expanding EEC in 1973. The EEA agreement between the EFTA and EC countries was an important intermediate step on the road to wider economic integration in Europe. Finland joined the European Union in January 1995.

Participation in the process of integration in Europe led to a major diversification of exports, with significant increases in the shares of the metal, engineering, clothing, electronic and chemical industries. The share of traditional forest industry products fell to about 40 % of the total. Some 44 % of Finnish exports go to EU countries like Germany, France, Great Britain, the Benelux countries, Italy and Sweden, followed by the United States and Japan. Trade with Russia and the other FSU countries has declined during the 1990s.

AGRICULTURE AND FORESTRY

Finnish farms have traditionally

A Finnish-made Valmet tractor in action drawing a silage harvester.

mixed agriculture with forestry. Smallholders have worked on the fields during the summer and in the forests during the winter. By the early 1950s, however, both branches had become extensively mechanised, thus freeing the labour urgently required by other branches of the economy. Between 1950 and 1990, the share of the labour force working in agriculture and forestry had declined from 46 to 8.6 per cent. The share of agriculture in gdp has also fallen, from 10 % at the beginning of the 1960s to 2.5 % in 1993.

Finnish agriculture is in a state of ferment as, with membership

This multi-purpose, microprocessor-operated machine is the latest aid to wood felling.

A Finnish paper-making machine at the Shotton Paper Mill in Scotland.

of the EU from the beginning of 1995, the country will have to bring its national agricultural policy into line with that of the EU. The main goal is that Finland will remain self-sufficient in respect to basic food products with as small a surplus as possible.

Animal husbandry continues to occupy a major role in Finnish agriculture, and production quotas for milk amount to almost 2.5 billion kilos. Farms have specialised in either dairy or beef cattle, pigs or chickens. Arable cultivation is concentrated in South Finland, where there are also market gardens and fur farms. Organic farming is not yet able to meet the ever growing demand. The most important arable crops are barley, oats, wheat, oleiferous plants, potatoes, sugar beet and rye. Lapland is considered the land of dairy cattle and the herding of some 215 000 head of reindeer. The goals of Finnish farming are the production of pure foodstuffs within a healthy environment.

About 70 % of Finland is covered by forests. The total stock of growing trees is over 1660 million m^3, with a yearly felling rate in recent times slightly under the annual increase of almost 70 million m^3. The forests are being threatened by acid rain, due largely to industrial pollution from other countries. The main species of tree are pine (40 % of the yearly growth), spruce (37 %) and birch, followed by significant numbers of aspen and alder. Felled wood is used either as roundwood in the sawmill, plywood and board industries, or as fibre in the pulp and paper industries. The use of wood as a fuel is coming back into fashion as a consequence of the new energy policy. Reforestation and the draining of wetlands increased considerably during the 1960s and 1970s. Draining measures were completed by the mid-1990s. As a result of the restructuring of agriculture, an ever greater number of forests have passed into the hands of non-farming owners. Although the state owns about 24 % of the forests, its stake in the wood industry remains minimal.

INDUSTRY

During the inter-war years Finnish industry was characterised by a division into export-market oriented industry, represented by the wood industry, and home-market oriented industry. This division remained until the 1950s. War reparations had fully utilised the capacity of the metal and engineering industries, whereas other branches had been hampered by rationing. Once reparation payments had been completed in 1952 the Soviet Union continued to place huge orders with the metal and engineering industries. As integration increased within Europe the wood and other industries began to receive orders from Western Europe.

Due to the country's massive forest resources and high-grade wood, exports from the pulp and

Above: Vaisala develops and manufactures measuring instruments for meteorological, environmental and industrial use. The picture shows a thin-film capacitive humidity sensor.

Examples of Finnish technology and industrial design. Above: Fiskars scissors, the most imitated Finnish product. Centre: helmet and ski binding. Below: Nokia's mobile telephone.

paper industries are still important. Finland is a major exporting country. About 70 % of the total production of the wood industry goes for export, accounting for almost 36 % of the total and 20 % of the value of industrially processed output. The share of high-grade paper and paper products within the industry is constantly increasing. It accounts for 27 % of the total output of Finnish industry.

Finland's most important branches of industry today are the metal and engineering industries, which account for about 33 % of total output and a similar percentage of total exports. Every third industrial worker is employed in these industries and some 45 % of output goes for export. There is little mining going on in Finland, yet the country is still an important producer of certain non-ferrous metals. The key branches in the metal industry are the high-tech production of steel and copper. The main products of the mechanical engineering industry are agricultural and forestry equipment, wood industry machines and equipment, fork trucks and lifts, consumer durables, electrical and electronic products. Finland is known throughout the world for its high-tech production of telephone exchanges, quality cars, mobile phones and consumer electronics. The mechanical engineering industry also produces lorries and special seagoing vessels, such as icebreakers, luxury liners, leisure-time submarines, and oil rigs often specially designed for operation under extreme climatic conditions.

The chemical industry has also grown and now accounts for 8 % of the processed value and 7 % of the gross value of industrial production. In addition to oil refining and fertilizers, this branch also has a significant output of techno-chemical and pharmaceutical products.

Thanks to successful design Finland has managed to acquire recognition abroad with such consumer products as clothing and footwear, furniture, utility and decorative glass, cutlery and jewellery. Due to high quality and competitive prices, the food, alcohol, tobacco and printing industries have landed considerable orders from abroad.

Domestic energy (mainly hydro-electric, wood- waste- and peat-produced) accounts for only 30 % of total consumption. Finland is thus heavily dependent upon energy imports. The share of oil has declined. Nowadays about 15 % of total energy consumption is produced by the country's four nuclear power stations, which account for about 32 % of electricity production.

CONSTRUCTION

As a result of migration, urbanisation and other social changes in the 1960s and 1970s, there was a major extension of the road, rail, harbour, canal and electricity networks, nuclear power stations were built, and a

In this promised age of cheap imports, Finland's textile industry struggles to maintain its market position through quality and design. Its greatest successes have been in leisure and sportswear.

massive housing programme introduced. To keep pace with industrial development many new factories, offices and public buildings were constructed. In the 1990s, however, investments have concentrated on refurbishing and maintenance. The share of the construction industry in gdp was 9 % at the beginning of the 1970s, with annual housing production in the region of 70 000 units, but this fell drastically during the 1990s.

DOMESTIC TRADE

The share of trade in total gdp has been 11 % and 15 % of employment. Productivity has increased as a result of rationalisation, self-service and improved storage and distribution facilities. Almost all food stores operate along self-service lines. Rapid urbanisation and increased car ownership have contributed to the demise of small shops in the more distant areas and their replacement by downtown multistore shopping malls, department stores and supermarkets. Two thirds of private consumption is channeled through the retail trade organised into a number of competing chains. Although fierce competition exists in the wholesale and retail trade in everyday goods, the recession has done much to induce the groups to cooperate. The state-owned Alko has a monopoly of the sale of wines, spirits and strong beers, though food shops are allowed to sell low-alcohol beers.

TRANSPORT AND COMMUNICATIONS

Finland's geographical location, dispersed population and highly variable climate set heavy technical and economic strains on transportation. The share of transport in gdp is 9 % and in emplyment 8 per cent.

Icebreakers ensure that the main harbours are kept open for shipping even during severe winters. The Saimaa Canal offers access from the Baltic to the east Finnish lake district for suitably-sized vessels. Otherwise traffic on the inland waterways, and also log floating, has been replaced by road transport. Most of Finland's merchant navy consists of luxury ferries for carrying passengers and freight, and highly automatised container and bulk cargo carriers.

Most of the country's approximately 75 000 km road network has been properly surfaced. An efficient fleet of snow ploughs keep the roads open during winter. The normal speed limits are 120 or 100 km/h on the motorways, 100 or 80 km/h on main roads, 80 km/h on subsidiary roads, and 50 or 40 km/h in built-up areas. During winter the speed limit is lowered on main roads to minimise accidents and prevent excessive wear-and-tear as studded tyres are not only permitted but are compulsory in wintertime. The driving test also requires experience on slippery roads. There are some 2,2 million cars in Finland, as well as hundreds of thousands of other motor vehicles. Together they constitute a serious threat to the railways. Of the 6 000 km of track in Finland, the most important sections (about 25 % of the total) have been electrified, the rest use diesel engines. All major towns operate their own local transport systems. Helsinki's, for instance, includes buses, trams, suburban trains and a metro.

The domestic airline network is one of the best in Europe. The state-owned Finnair flies to all the major industrial countries, the longest hauls being to Japan and the United States.

Finland's trunk-call telephone network is completely digitalised and also about 60 % of the local-call network. About 60 % of the population are subscribers to fixed telephone networks and another 10 % are within the mobile phone network. Finland has the next highest density of mobile-phone users in the world after Sweden. The telephone network and other telecommunication connections are, internationally, top grade. A considerable number of people are working with data communications and companies are increasingly using public switched data networks in their operations.

BANKING AND INSURANCE

The central bank, the Bank of Finland, has been set four main tasks to perform in the national economy. As an economic policy decision maker it strives to maintain a stable exchange rate as well as a stable price level within the country. As the currency authority it ensures the country's external liquidity, ie. that there is sufficient currency to pay for imports and service the foreign debt. As the bankers' bank, it can advance credit to banks in difficulties. Being in charge of money it ensures that there is a sufficiency of banknotes and coins in circulation. A significant part of the payments infrastructure of the banks in Finland is managed through a computerised system of account transfers. The operations of the Bank of Finland are supervised by the Parliamentary Supervisory Board. A stable exchange rate has been the long term aim of Finland. This had to be relinquished after the 1991 devaluation and since 1992 the markka has been allowed to float freely. By 1996, however, the value of the markka had returned to its pre-devaluation level. It is also the aim of the country to participate in the creation of a single EU currency.

Banks in Finland offer a wide range of services and may participate in a variety of money market operations. National differences between banking systems are, however, disappearing, and in most countries today there are normal commercial banks and specialist banks. The use of cheques in Finland is far rarer than elsewhere. The share of deposit banks in outstanding, domestic credit is over 50 %. As in many other countries depositors enjoy account protection. Banks are supervised

Leaders of the world's mints chose the Finnish ten mark coin as the most beautiful coin in circulation in 1992–94. Designed by sculptor Antti Neuvonen, the coin is of the two-metal type with the centre from aluminium bronze and the outer rim from copper nickel. Rahapaja Oy has been very successful minting coins for the overseas market, and its main countries of export in 1994 were Thailand, Namibia, Latvia and Israel.

and inspected far more than other companies. Problems within the national economy are felt by the banks when their customers run into difficulties. The recession in Finland, following the collapse of exports to the former Soviet Union, was the worst in any industrialised country in peace-time. No banking system could have avoided difficulties in such a situation. In Finland this led to the merging of most of the savings banks, the segmentation of one of the largest of them among the other banks, the sale of STS to Kansallis-Osake-Pank-ki, the collapse of some of the cooperative savings funds, and finally the merger of the two largest commercial banks, Kansallis-Osake-Pankki and Suomen Yhdyspankki, to form Merita. The whole banking sector has undergone severe restructuring. As bank competition these days is global, even major mergers are no longer considered restrictive. Credit and bank cards are much in use, and proof of identity is required in shops and elsewhere for purchases of over FIM 300.

In addition to the banks, another important source of credit is the insurance companies. Insurance companies predict the timing of paying pensions and settling claims, and invest the premium income according to

Ever more Finns acquire a weekend or summer cottage in the countryside in addition to their town dwelling. Shares in Lapp skiing centres or holiday condominiums in the sunny south are also popular.

the type of insurance involved. Premium income comes from voluntary and compulsory insurance policies. The Finnish employees' pension scheme is different from other countries in that although it is decided upon by the state, the assets are invested in private pension insurance companies and funds. The individual employee has no say over how his premium payments are invested. Voluntary pension schemes are becoming increasingly popular. Insurance companies are supervised by the Insurance Department of the Ministry for Social Affairs and Health.

Trading in the stocks and shares of companies quoted on the Helsinki Stock Exchange is conducted by banks and authorised brokerage firms. The book-entry system prevails in Finland. Foreign investors play a major role in stock exchange trading. The importance of investment funds has increased.

THE PUBLIC SECTOR

The growth in overall production and services is due to the extension of publicly-financed activities. The civil service, defence, education and research, hospital and health services, and social security are an integral part of Finnish society. There are considerably more people working in the services than in industry.

Public services are maintained out of taxation by either the state or the local municipalities. The state aids municipalities in proportion to their incomes.

The most important direct tax is that levied by local authorities on all residents, the rate being under 20 % of their incomes. State income tax is progressive, and at most the rate is slightly under 40 % of taxable income. The rates for the state income and property taxes, as well as the local tax, are determined annually. In addition, there is also a tax-like social security charge on incomes.

The main indirect tax is VAT, the rate of which, with certain exceptions, is 22 % on the retail price. Excise taxes are imposed on fuel, tobacco, alcoholic beverages and services. The motor vehicle tax is one of the highest in the world. Stamp duty is another important source of income for the state. The importance of customs duties, has radically declined.

The state's share of direct taxation is about 60 %, the local authorities 25 %, and the remaining 14 % consists largely of social security contributions. The trend in tax policy has been towards indirect taxation. Different forms of income transfers and benefits to individuals and companies alike play an important part in the public economy. In addition to public housing programmes, various interest-subsidised loans account for a major part of both central and local government expenditure. The largest items of state and

Foreign trade 1994

IMPORTS by region

- EC 43,6 %
- EFTA 18,1 %
- Other countries 17,5 %
- Developing countries 8,1 %
- Other Europe 12,6 %

IMPORTS by use of goods

- Raw materials 60,3 %
- Crude oil 5,4 %
- Fuels 4,3 %
- Investment goods 14,3 %
- Consumer goods 20,5 %
- Other articles 0,7 %

EXPORTS by region

- EC 46,5 %
- EFTA 16,7 %
- Other countries 13,8 %
- Developing countries 10,6 %
- Other Europe 12,4 %

EXPORTS by industries

- Paper and graphic industry 26,8 %
- Chemical industry 10,2 %
- Basic metal industry 8,3 %
- Metal product and machine industry 36,2 %
- Textile, clothing and leather industry 2,2 %
- Other industries 7,1 %
- Wood industry 9,2 %

munici-pal expenses are for education, cultural activities and social security.

CONSUMPTION AND THE STANDARD OF LIVING

The share of food in private consumption is about 20 %, (18 % without the inclusion of alcoholic beverages). The share rises to 25 % when drinks and meals outside the home are taken into account. Expenditure on alcohol and tobacco accounts for over 3 per cent. The average size of dwellings is approximately 75 m^2 and the space per inhabitant is about 32 m^2. Thanks to a socially-oriented housing programme few people any more have to endure cramped living conditions. Nowadays over 65 % of the people own their own homes and some 26 % live in council houses. There are, in addition, some 400 000 leisure-time second homes. Housing absorbs about 19 % of household income. Finnish homes are well-upholstered and saturation point has been reached with many household appliances. The share of transport (eg. cars) and electronics (for amusement and education) in consumption is 22 %, with recreation, culture and hobbies accounting for about 9 per cent.

Finnish consumer protection law establishes the general principles governing the sale and marketing of goods and services, and regulates the relationship between buyers and sellers. A special board exists to handle without charge consumer complaints concerning the sale and marketing of consumer goods. The sale and marketing of real estate and apartments is also regulated by law. Another law determines responsibility for products and regulates the relationship between the consumer and the manufacturer and seller of the goods.

The public sector in Finland also provides free basic education, excellent further educational facilities, a virtually free national health service, extensive social security, subsidised public transport and cultural amenities.

BALANCING THE NATIONAL ECONOMY

It has been difficult trying to balance the national economy in the 1990s as the country's foreign debt has grown rapidly. The employment situation deteriorated and at its worst in the mid-1990s there were about 500 000 unemployed, almost 20 % of the labour force. Even so there was a shortage of skilled workers in certain fields. The annual rise in the cost of living index dropped from 4.1 % in 1991 to 1.1 % in 1994. Food prices fell slightly after Finland joined the EU. The balance of payments has long shown a deficit, but the growth in exports has alleviated the situation. The economic downturn has meant difficulties in balancing the budget as the fall in tax revenues was greater than anticipated.

SOCIAL SECURITY

After decades of steady progress, Finland's system of social security is now one of the finest in the world. No less than 18.5 % of the budget goes on social expenditure. In 1995 FIM 48.7 million was allotted in the state budget for social security.

The system covers all potential social risks, and its most important aspect is social insurance. This includes national and employment pension schemes, accident and health insurance, and unemployment assistance and benefits. Support services for families, the elderly and handicapped continue to be in great demand.

HEALTH INSURANCE

The health insurance scheme administered by the National Pensions Institution covers all people residing in Finland, offering them medical attention, laboratory and x-ray examination, and even physiotherapy for a nominal fee. Patients are

Rehabilitation is of primary importance in health care. This is a kinetic measuring apparatus for assessing the straightening abilities of patients suffering from chronic back trouble. The results are used in planning physiotherapy programmes.

required to pay part of the cost of prescribed medicines, except in cases of the chronically sick when they are free.

A small charge, roughly equivalent to running costs, is levied on hospital treatment. All health and hospital expenses, as well as necessary travel expenses, over a certain minimum sum are refunded.

Part of the cost of private medical attention and examination is also covered. All those born in 1956 and after are included within the dental treatment scheme, likewise war veterans. All those of working age receive a daily allowance amounting to 80 % of their salary when ill. And for those not actually in employment, a minimum daily allowance is paid.

A maternity allowance is paid on the same basis as the daily sickness allowance. This is paid for a period of ten months, part of which is parental leave when either the mother or father can look after their baby. The allowance is paid even if the mother returns to work prior to the end of her maternity leave.

PENSION INSURANCE

The normal pensionable age in Finland for both men and women is 65 years, although in many occupations it is lower. Upon reaching pensionable age, almost everybody receives the national pension in addition to an employ-ment pension if they have been working. The object of the latter is to ensure continuance of the same standard of living enjoyed whilst working. The amount of national pension depends on the wealth and income of the individual. Pensioners with very large incomes are no longer entitled to recive the national pension.

The amount of the employment pension is directly related to previous earnings and the number of years worked. The maximum employment pension, 60 % of salary, is paid after 40 years in work. The larger the employment pension, the smaller the national pension. No upper limit is set on pensions in Finland.

Central and local authority employees, and those working in other public bodies, have their own pension schemes that are very similar to the employment pension scheme.

UNEMPLOYMENT ASSISTANCE

Nearly all organised workers belong to voluntary unemployment benefit funds operated by the trade unions. In order to draw unemployment benefit from the fund a worker must have been a member for at least six months. A ceiling is set to the annual benefits paid and to those paid over a three-year period. The funds are financed by the employers, the state, and less importantly the members.

The unemployment benefit paid by the state to those not

There are several rehabilitation institutes for disabled war veterans. Seated volley ball has been developed especially for amputee patients.

covered by the funds is roughly proportionate to those in a comparable occupation. It is only enough to cover very basic needs.

ACCIDENT INSURANCE

Employers are compelled by law to insure their employees against loss of earnings and medical costs incurred as a result of accidents at work or occupational diseases. Third party motor insurance is compulsory for all motor vehicle owners.

FAMILY ALLOWANCES

Child benefit is paid to the parents of all children under 17 residing in Finland. An increased benefit is paid on children under the age of three. Municipalities operate day-care centres for the pre-school aged children of working parents. About one third of all children are looked after in the homes of local-authority supervised and approved child minders. Families with an under three-year-old child, managed at home or by a private child minder, are paid a monthly allowance. There is considerable variation in the provision of day-care facilities by local authorities, and although required by law to provide places for all pre-school children, there are still not enough of them.

A baby having a regular check-up at the clinic.

Families with a handicapped or seriously ill child under 16 are entitled to home-care assistance. A mother, whose child does not receive financial assistance from the father, receives a state maintenance benefit.

All expectant mothers receive a maternity kit: either a parcel of baby clothes and materials or money, the former being worth more than the latter. These days there are even paternity kits available.

CARE OF THE ELDERLY

Municipalities arrange many different services, at a nominal charge, to help elderly people with such everyday chores as cleaning, cooking, shopping, running errands and transportation. Then there are special centres where senior citizens can obtain information and meet people. Some of these function in conjunction with old people's homes. Apartment blocks have also been built for the elderly which take into account their special needs. Similar places have been built for the handicapped.

HEALTH CARE

HEALTH CENTRES

Local authorities, either alone or together with neighbouring areas, are required under the national health service to maintain health centres.

Their function is to provide the local population with medical services, first aid, antenatal and

Families with pre-school children have a constitutional right to daycare.

Town and municipal sanitation services keep the roads clean and free from snow.

postnatal clinical services, and the school health care service. One of their most important tasks is to give advice and check the health of expectant and nursing mothers, and regularly check the health of the children from the time they are born to when they go to school. So effective is this system that Finland has an extremely low level of child mortality. Virtually all children attend the clinics for regular medical checks, innoculations, etc, the details of which are entered in their health cards, which accompany them throughout school. Health centres are also responsible for organising the local ambulance service.

Although health centres provide the basic medical services required, there are also private centres where authorised doctors practice medicine, often in addition to their hospital duties.

HOSPITALS

In many health centres there are also wards, but these are mainly intended for chronic patients. The centre's function is to decide whether a patient should go for hospital treatment or examination by a specialist. The country is divided into 21 hospital districts, and the muncipalities within the district are responsible for the maintenance of their central hospital. The state contributes towards the cost in proportion to the means of the district in question.

Central hospitals must provide

wards for the treatment of most general diseases. Doctors, though not interns, must be specialists. Five of the central hospitals are university teaching hospitals.

Smaller local units supplement the services of the district central hospitals, and are required to provide treatment in three specialist fields. They are also maintained by the local authorities, but there is no nationwide system as they are established on a voluntary basis.

In addition to the central and local hospitals, there are mental institutions, military and penal hospitals, etc. The maintenance of hospital services has been traditionally thought of as a charge on the community, so there are few private ones. There are some 430 hospitals in Finland, providing 11–12 beds per thousand inhabitants.

PATIENTS

Patients are hospitalised only on the recommendation of a health centre GP, except in the case of accidents and emergencies. In this way the most intensive use is made of hospital resources. Patients are normally admitted to their local hospital.

ENVIRONMENTAL HEALTH

Environmental health is the responsibility of the local authorities, and involves environmental hygiene, control of foodstuffs and poisons, occupational health and veterinary medicine.

Great stress is placed upon food hygiene and safety: control of the production, storage and sale of food, and supervising the health of those handling food. The relevant EU legislation has been applied in Finland since the beginning of 1995. Environmental health also covers drinking water, clean air and noise control. A nationwide system has been introduced for the disposal of problem wastes.

HOUSING POLICY

Housing production clearly reflects the rapid urbanisation of Finland that has taken place since the early 1950s. So great was the pressure that over half of existing housing was built during the last thirty years. The recession in the 1990s has, however, considerably reduced annual housing production.

The goal of development area policy is to balance out regional inequalities and stem the flow of rural people to the southern conurbations.

Local authorities are responsible for the overall living environment. All building is in accordance with an approved local plan, subject to the availability of capital and land ownership relations. Residents' associations and private citizens have shown a growing interest in communal planning, due to the increased importance of the quality of life. By improving the level of their surroundings they also improve the quality of their houses and apartments.

Rentable dwellings account for over 26 % of the total. Families with children, old people and students can obtain a housing allowance to help them maintain a reasonable standard of living. Living costs in Finland are quite high, largely due to the need to build to withstand arctic conditions, but also because of strict safety regulations.

The law on consumer protection also applies to the sale and marketing of houses and flats.

LABOUR POLICY

Labour policy concerns employer-employee relations, work safety and manpower questions. Employers and employees are required to co-operate to maintain and develop work safety. Special work safety committees exist in larger companies with representatives appointed by both sides. These either carry out their own safety inspections, or participate in those made by the state or local authorities.

Work safety regulations cover such matters as work place

lighting, temperature, noise levels and ventilation, safety devices on machinery, civil defence equipment, advice and instructions, and organising first aid.

Although the 8 hour day, 40 hour week is normal, many work less, as for example 36 hours in a regular three-shift working week. Parents with babies or children in their first year at school have the possibility of working shorter hours. Employees are entitled to a minimum of 2 days holiday for each month worked; some have more and also a week-long winter holiday. The content of employment contracts between employers and employees is regulated by law. Collective bargaining agreements between the employers' confederations and the trade unions prescribe wage and salary levels, social benefits, period of notice, etc. General agreements on wages and salaries are mostly negotiated annually.

Over half of the total number of houses in Finland were built during the last thirty years. The picture is of one of the western suburbs in Espoo in the greater metropolitan area of Helsinki.

THE CHURCH

Almost exactly 85,6 % of Finns belong to the Evangelical Lutheran Church. This figure does not include those members of the church who have been placed in institutions or left the country.

Although Christianity had probably reached Finland by the end of the first millennium AD, it was not until the 12th century that the Roman Catholic Church became established. This followed the so-called crusade of the Swedish king Eric and his English-born bishop Henry to south-west Finland. The influence of the Orthodox Church spread into the country from the east, gathering under its wing all those who lived in what is now east Karelia. Thus religious and cultural boundaries deepened the country's division into two spheres of influence: Novgorod and Russia on the one side and Swedish Finland on the other.

Following the Reformation in Scandinavia and Finland in the 16th century, Finland became Lutheran. Complete freedom of religion, however, was not guaranteed until 1923. Nowadays there are 594 Lutheran parishes in the country with

Many of Finland's beautiful old wooden churches have survived. The one in the picture is in Vimpeli.

4.3 million members, making it the world's third largest Lutheran church.

The clearly secular character of Finnish society owes much to the strong element of individualism in Protestantism. Nevertheless, the great majority of Finns still value the church and its works, and use it at the main junctures of their lives. Over 90 % of all children are baptised and confirmed. Only a few adult members prefer to be married in a registry office, and many non-members desire a church funeral. Religious programmes on the radio and TV are very popular.

Women have been ordained in Finland since 1988. The picture shows the youth curate of Tuusula at a confirmation class camp.

The church most easily reaches children, youth and the elderly. It also offers family guidance and distress phone services.

Parishes have a wide degree of financial and operational independence, electing their own priests and parish officials. The administrative bodies are elected every four years.

The 594 parishes are divided into eight dioceses, one of which is Swedish-speaking, each with its own bishop and chapter. Bishops are appointed by the president from a short list of three proposed by the chapter. Turku, the capital of Finland until 1812, is still the seat of the archbishop, though the National Ecclesiastical Board, which manages the administration and

finances of the church, is in Helsinki.

The highest decision-making body is the Church Assembly or Synod, one-third of whose members are clergy and two-thirds laity. Its tasks include deciding upon church operations and finances, approving ecclesiastical books and entering into agreements with other churches. Another important function is proposing amendments to the Ecclesiastical Act which must then go to parliament for approval. Parliament can either accept or reject them, but not change them, and in practice always approves them. After a heated debate the assembly finally accepted the ordination of women in 1986, and two years later parliament gave its assent to the proposed amendment to the Ecclesiatical Act. The same year the first female theological graduates were ordained, thus enabling them to perform all church duties. As yet no woman has been consecrated as a bishop, although the office is open to them.

Over the last century the bond between church and state has so weakened that the former is nowadays virtually independent of the latter. One important link remains: parishes have the right

Interior of the church of Valamo monastery in Heinävesi.

to levy taxes. This is collected by the inland revenue office along with other income taxes. Non-members of the Evangelical Lutheran and Orthodox churches do not pay church tax, though companies must. This is considered as payment for such church-provided communal services as the maintenance of the local registers of births, deaths and marriages for church members and the upkeep of graveyards.

Children receive or are excused from religious instruction at school in accordance with their parents' beliefs.

With a membership of almost 60 000, the Orthodox Church is the second largest church in Finland. Its earlier centres are in those parts of Karelia now in Russia. For long the church suffered from the dispersion of its congregation throughout the country as a result of the war, but nowadays it is again thriving and vigorous. Its importance in Finland is far greater than its modest membership presupposes.

After the two main churches, the most significant religious group in Finland, at least in respect to the activity of its members, is the Pentecostal movement. As its congregations are not registered, it is estimated to have some 50 000 members. The other groups are much smaller and include some 4000 Roman Catholics, 12 500 members of the Finnish Free Church, 5000 Adventists, etc. The Jewish community has about a thousand members, the Islamic community slightly less, and there are about 13 000 Jehovah's Witnesses. Some 600 000 people, almost 12 % of the population, do not belong to any religious order, although some of them are members of unregistered religious groups.

SCHOOLS AND EDUCATION

Compulsory schooling takes place in Finland between the ages of 7 and 16, and there is additional provision for voluntary education for pre-school children. Basic education is given to all children upon reaching the age of seven in comprehensive schools consisting of nine compulsory forms and an optional tenth. Further education is voluntary, either in the three-year upper secondary schools or 2–5-year courses in vocational schools. Higher education is provided by the universities.

Education, science and culture account for 17–18 % of total government expenditure.

PRE-SCHOOL EDUCATION
It is the task of the Ministry for Social Affairs and Health and the local authorities to arrange day care for the under seven-year-old children of working parents. This is organised either in municipal day-care centres or in the homes of approved childminders. The latter cope with about one third of total demand. As over three quarters of the mothers of under school-age children go to work, there is a desperate shortage of places in municipal day-care centres, especially in the larger towns.

Another function of day care is to augment home upbringing and ensure the balanced development of a child's personality.

Applicants for day-care centre teacher training are required to have matriculated. The course lasts three years, sufficient time

Organised hobbies are a feature of kindergarden life. These young actors are king and queen in the school play.

The Finnish school system

to provide potential teachers with a thorough theoretical background.

COMPREHENSIVE SCHOOLS
The aim of comprehensives is to provide a socio-ethical and aesthetic education in addition to the traditional subjects. Thus a good memory is no longer so important as the ability to study and think, and develop one's personality.

Although a comprehensive school may have a pre-school form for 6-year-old children, it is normally divided into two parts. At the junior level (forms 1–6) all children receive exactly the same education, given by their form teachers except in the case of languages. At the senior level

	Monday	Tuesday	Wednesday	Thursday	Friday
9–10	Geography	Finnish	Rk	Finnish	Math
10–11	Math	Finnish	Geography	Geography	Finnish
11–12	Art	Music	Math	Finnish	Civics
12–13	Art	Math	History	English	Handicrafts
13–14	Pe	English	Pe	Pe	Handicrafts
14–15		History			

6th form comprehensive school timetable.

(forms 7–9) teachers teach their own subjects. The junior level week is between 20 and 26 hours, and the senior level 30 hours.

The comprehensive aims at providing children with a general education. Compulsory subjects at the junior level are mathematics, religious knowledge, environmental studies, Finnish or Swedish (depending on the child's mother tongue), foreign languages (mostly English), history and social studies, civics, biology and geography, physical education, music, art and handicrafts.

The same subjects are also taught at the senior level with the exception of environmental studies. New compulsory subjects are chemistry and physics, home economics, and the second official language. Senior level pupils can also take such optional extras as economics, other foreign languages, agriculture or computer studies. When the syllabus was reformed in the mid-1990s, the emphasis was on increasing alternative and optional subjects.

By international standards Finns place great emphasis on studying foreign languages – work on the first one starts in the third form – but rather less on their mother tongue and mathematics. Pupils also receive study and career guidance, as well as regular extra tuition and counselling if required.

As parts of Finland are very sparsely populated, rural schools are small, with only two or three teachers, and have joint forms in which the age difference may be as great as four years. An effort is being made to apply the teaching advantage of small forms to the towns, and also to decentralise decision making in respect to the organisation of teaching.

Training for comprehensive school form teachers is given in the universities, and there are seven Finnish-language and one Swedish-language faculties, each with its own demonstration school. The course lasts 4–5 years, and for junior and senior level subject teachers 5–6 years.

The leading publishers offer a wide choice of textbooks. Comprehensive school textbooks are

The Heureka Science Centre in Vantaa is a favourite among comprehensive school children. Here they are studying the movement of a chaotic pendulum.

chosen by the teachers.

The municipality is responsible for arranging general education. Tuition, materials and school meals are all free, and if the journey to school is over 5 km then there is free transportation. Local authorities receive aid from the state to maintain schools in accordance with their means. This can be as high as 100 %.

SENIOR SECONDARY EDUCATION
There are two types of senior secondary education in Finland: the three-year senior secondary school, *lukio*, similar to the British sixth form, which represents the traditional academic line, and the vocational schools. One of the problems with the present system of vocational education is its fragmentation into many

different lines of study.

Senior secondary education is now based on modules or courses, each one lasting 38 study hours. There may be several courses in the same subject before the final examination. Pupils study the following subjects: Finnish and Swedish, 1–3 foreign languages, mathematics, physics, chemistry, geography, biology, psychology, reglious knowledge, art or music, physical education and hygiene. Some of them are compulsory, others optional. Careers counselling is also given. There are special *lukios* for those with a special talent for music, art or physical education.

Nowadays, most senior secondary schools are run by the muncipality, and only a few by the state or privately. Since 1994, these schools have functioned with or without the traditional form structure.

At the end of the three years, the knowledge and abilities of pupils are tested in the nationwide "student exam" or matriculation held in spring and autumn. Matriculation is the basic requirement for a higher education, and every year there are some 40 000 new students. As there are only 18 000 university places each year, some of which are reserved, many of these newly-qualified students must seek a vocational education or go to work.

In vocational education, pupils choose a basic line from 25 different trades and professions. Each of these is divided into two stages, a general and specialised phase. The year-long general phase has the same content for all pupils, after which they specialise in their specific trade. These specialised courses vary in level and last from one to four years. For example, in car mechanics a pupil can qualify as a skilled fitter after the short course, a technician after the middle course, and an engineer

White-capped students celebrate the official first day of spring (May 1st) with songs, champagne and balloons.

The 350th anniversary of Helsinki University was celebrated in 1990 with no less than five degree conferment ceremonies. Here the procession moves from the university building to Helsinki Cathedral.

after the longest course. There are 240 lines varying in content and level to choose from, plus a dozen or so special study lines.

All those who have completed the longest specialised courses are entitled to continue their education at a university.

Pupils undergoing upper secondary education can apply for non-returnable study grants.

About half of the vocational schools are run by the municipalities, a third by the state and the rest privately. The state, however, covers between 70 and 100 % of all their expenses.

HIGHER EDUCATION

Finland's first university, the Royal Academy of Turku, was founded in 1640 when the country was part of Sweden, and transferred to Helsinki in 1828 when that town became the new capital. In 1990 it thus celebrated its 350th anniversary. Prior to independence two other institutions of higher education, one technical and one commercial, were established, and immediately afterwards two new universities.

With the aim of regional equality in mind, several other universities have been established since the 1950s. Nowadays there are 17 universities and four art academies, with a total student population of 80 000. The largest is the University of Helsinki (about

26 000 students), then come the universities of Turku and Tampere (each with almost 10 000 students), the University of Technology in Espoo, near Helsinki (over 9000 students), Oulu University (over 8000 students) and Jyväskylä University (about 7000 students).

Each year the universities take about 18 000 new students, some of whom come up from the vocational schools. The number trying to get in greatly exceeds the number of places, often many times over. The basic criteria for entrance are the senior secondary (or vocational) school leaving report, matriculation grades and success in the entrance exams. Over half of the undergraduates are women.

The universities are directly under the Ministry of Education and state owned. They are, however, self-governing, and the administrative bodies of some have representatives not only of the professors, but also the other teachers, staff, and even the students.

Students may apply for state grants or state-guaranteed loans from the banks to finance their education. Via the students' unions, the state also subsidises student hostels, health care and meals.

An effort has been made to closely relate scientific education to professional occupations. The number of study weeks required for a degree is the best indication of the breadth of study. A study week means 40 hours of independent study. In most fields students must first obtain a basic (Bachelor's or Master's) degree in general, specific and in-depth studies. This usually requires 160 study weeks or 4–5 years of study. After the first degree students can go on, straight away if they wish, to study for their Licenciate or PhD.

The number of students in the arts and social sciences has been deliberately reduced in favour of the natural sciences, technology and medicine. As teaching and research are closely related, this change is also clearly reflected in research. The scientific level of research is the responsibility of the professors. The number of professors is divided between the disciplines as follows: arts and social sciences 36 %, natural sciences 28 %, technology 18 % and medicine 18 %.

Higher education is open to all at the numerous summer universities held every year. Only part of the tuition is at university

An exacting entrance examination must be passed before being admitted to university, and only about 35 % make it. The picture is of the university library, in Senate Square, Helsinki, and considered to be the most beautiful work of the architect Carl Ludvig Engel.

level, the rest is to supplement vocational or senior secondary education.

RESEARCH

Research accounted for about 3,1 % of the national budget in 1994. The Technology Development Centre (TEKES) receives about a quarter of state research expenditure. Public and private sector R&D accounts for over 2 % of gdp. Over half of this comes from private sources. Although industry operates its own research institutes, it also finances university research programmes, particularly technological research which absorbs over half of the available funds.

Public sector research funds are used to finance university research and the work of the 25 ministry-run research institutes. Of this about a quarter goes to the universities, which accounts for about 70 % of their expenditure on research. Some 60 % of university research work is primary, 30 % applied, and 10 % development in which industry also participates. About 85 % of the country's scientific literature is in the university libraries.

The administration of scientific work is centred in the Academy of Finland under the Ministry of Education. It is divided into seven councils representing the different branches of science. It finances research projects, normally for set periods. Most of the researchers work in the universities, who receive about a tenth of their research budget from the Academy. The Academy is also responsible for scientific policy making.

Historical and folklore research in Finland has been of major national importance, and one field of continued interest is that of the Finno-Ugrian languages. Philosophical research has been the most successful internationally. Also work in the social sciences has widened during the last three decades.

Research traditions are of great importance in a small country. In mathemathics, for example, one can talk of the Finnish school of function theory. Mathematics, unlike the natural sciences, does not demand huge investments, nevertheless research in the latter is at an international level. Likewise medical research, where notable work has been done into the use

A cryostat constructed in the Low Temperature Laboratory of the Helsinki University of Technology. The aparatus is used for investigating the properties of rotating superfluid ^{3}He. At low temperatures helium turns into a superfluid; the liquid has no viscosity and some vortices are created on the surface of the liquid. When experiments are made, the temperature of the inner parts of the cryostat is 1mK (about − 273.15°C).

of interferon to combat cancer and virus infections. The North Karelia Project concerning the effect of life style on health (more specifically, the role of food in causing hypertension) has received international recognition.

Finland has also been a pioneer in agricultural and forestry research, especially in such fields as forest type theory and resource evaluation.

Part of the research work done in technology and engineering has been in collaboration with Finnish industry. International recognition has been given for work in the development of chrome steel, corrosion studies and copper flash-smelting processes.

The leading figures in Finnish research today include Georg Henrik von Wright, Jaakko Hintikka and Raimo Tuomela in philosophy and logic, Jaakko Paunio in economics, Erik Allardt in sociology, Olli Lehto in mathematics, Kari Cantell for his work on interferon, Olli Lounasmaa in physics and Martti Tiuri in communications.

ADULT EDUCATION

Alongside full-time education aimed at a degree or some other qualification, there exists a very diverse and informal system of voluntary adult education. Originally this was intended to provide both a general education and stimulate leisure-time activities, often in preparation for work in the community. However, during the 1980s increasing emphasis was placed on vocational training.

Adult education is arranged through different associations and organisations, and is partly state supported. Most of the courses are organised through a nationwide network of civic and workers' institutes, with more than 600 000 students. The first institutes were established in 1899, and most are maintained by the local authorities. Courses, mainly held in the evenings, are of a general educational, social or leisure-oriented nature. Some institutes offer senior secondary school courses for those going to work, but only in exceptional circumstances can examination certificates be given.

A general, social and vocational education is also provided in folk institutes (established in 1899) and folk academies. These are residential and take about 7000 students a year. Some of them are entitled to give upper secondary school leaving certificates.

Many political parties and trade unions have ideological and educational associations that arrange lectures, courses and seminars. They have also established numerous study centres to further their activities. Working methods vary, but perhaps the most popular are the study circles which embrace

Although Toimela is a private adult educational institute it still receives state assistance. It teaches languages, mathematics, art, gymnastics and music. The picture shows an art student at work.

some 20 000 students each year.

There are also about 130 music schools with some 50 000 students, and 12 sports institutes, four of which produce physical education instructors.

Correspondence schools offer both general and vocational education, the latter often organised by industry and business. Radio and TV courses are increasing and extremely popular.

Essential to adult education are the extensive lending facilities of the state-supported libraries, and the lectures, exhibitions and other cultural events which they arrange.

Employment courses for those facing unemployment or already unemployed, or in need of further training or retraining, are given in vocational course centres. With the rapid restructuring of industrial and business life, a growing number of people of working age need to attend retraining courses. These centres are maintained jointly by the educational and employment authorities. Instruction is free, travel and accommodation expenses and meals are paid for, and participants receive a daily allowance.

The open university is rapidly expanding, and the universities maintain supplementary educational centres to coordinate these activities. Because the country is so vast, auxiliary forms of education such as the telephone and computer are used. Multiform education is provided as 39 institutes, and some 50 000 students are enrolled in the open university.

Vocational education administered by the educational authorities reaches almost 500 000 adults each year.

CULTURE

The roots of Finnish culture lie deep in prehistory, in the customs and beliefs of the ancient Finns. These are most graphically portrayed in the national epic, the *Kalevala*, compiled by Elias Lönnrot from the oral memories of rune singers in the early 19th century.

Finland's cultural development has also been affected by its long association with Sweden and the Roman Catholic church, ancient trading links with Germany and the Baltic states, and the Eastern influence, seen most clearly in the role of the Orthodox church in Karelia. The spread of new cultural influences in the western areas was facilitated by more populous village settlements, whereas the scattered communities in Karelia favoured the retention of ancient traditions.

With only some 15 % of borrowed words in the language, this might attest to cultural continuity, but on closer analysis these words have come from all directions, from the Baltic, Sweden and Russia. The absorption of these influences over the centuries can be recognised in the multiple nuances of modern Finnish culture.

FOLK TRADITIONS AND FESTIVALS

In folk tradition, the relationship of Finns to nature traces its origin back to pagan times, when they worshipped the many gods and spirits that personified nature and the elements. The greatest of these was *Ukko*, god of thunder and lightning, and his wife *Rauni*, mother nature, who together took care of the weather and the seasons. He lives on in modern Finnish in the word for thunder, *ukkonen*. Ancient Finns were not particularly worried about these gods, for when trouble faced the tribe or family, there was always the wise man, the shaman, *Väinämöinen*, to intercede on their behalf.

It was impossible to separate nature from its religious context. The old beliefs were so much a part of everyday life that Christianity found it difficult to counter them. Christianity spread to Finland from both east and west towards the end of the first millennium AD. The ancient rituals associated with nature were transposed into celebrations of Christian feasts and saints.

Although the Reformation in the 1520s officially swept the old Catholic saints away, the ancient legends and traditions survived and even thrived among the

In the old days a variety of decorative wooden implements were given the bride by the groom. The picture shows a mangle board, distaff head and a woven *käspaikka* or hand towel, which was also used in religious ceremonies.

common people. For example, on December 26th, *Tapaninpäivä*, it was the custom to ride in sledges drawn by foals harnessed for the first time.

This was, after all, St. Stephen's day, the patron saint of horses. July 27th, Sleepyhead Day, *Unikeonpäivä*, commemorated the legend of the seven martyrs of Ephesus who fled from the emperor Decius and spent the years from 249–447 asleep in a cave. According to the custom, anyone who slept late on this day would be tired for the rest of the year. This day is still celebrated in Hanko and Naantali.

Laskiainen, Shrove Tuesday, is celebrated seven weeks before Easter, but many of the customs associated with it are very ancient and concern work, signifying the last day of the annual work cycle. Easter, despite its Christian origin, contains elements linking it to ancient Finnish customs, such as preventing witches and evil spirits harming the cattle by lighting bonfires. Certain areas still have their Easter bonfires, but mostly the tradition has changed. Nowadays, young girls, dressed as witches and armed with willow twigs decorated with coloured paper and feathers, go from house to house wishing people good luck and prosperity.

Bonfires at Midsummer, St. John the Baptist's Day, *Juhannus*, are strangely thought to be early Christian in origin, but many old folk traditions are associated with this magical nightless day. It is the celebration of growth, fertility. In most areas doorways

Of all the traditional Midsummer bonfires, the biggest in the Helsinki area is at the Seurasaari openair museum.

Folk costumes occupy a particularly prominent place in Sami culture.

are still decorated with young birch trees and magnificent Midsummer poles are raised in the Åland Islands. Cattle were bedecked with garlands of flowers and young maidens placed a sprig of nine herbs under their pillows so they would dream of their future bridegrooms. Naked girls rolled in the dewy grass because they believed it to be a powerful ahprodisiac, and when they looked into a pool they would see the face of their beloved. Many of these old customs have been kept alive because they provide people with fun and amusement.

Christmas, *joulu*, was, and still is, the most important feast of the year. Originally, it signified the completion of the harvest year, and thus is celebrated with such traditional foods as salmon, roast pork, stockfish, sausages, vegetable casseroles, rice pudding, prune pies, and home-brewed beer. The idea of the Christmas tree spread rapidly in the last century, and is perhaps the most important element of the Finnish Christmas.

Originally, the Finnish Father Christmas, *joulupukki*, took the form of a goat, or of a man disguised as a goat, who went from house to house throwing presents in through the doorways. However, following a children's radio programme in 1927, the present day Father Christmas, with his Korvatunturi home in Finnish Lapland, took shape to the lasting delight of children throughout the world.

Folklore traditions and customs survived into the early part of this century, and even folk art retained its original forms. It took time before industrialisation penetrated the distant rural areas, so peasant culture survived intact. The life of the peasant was tied to the seasons, and his close observation of nature gave rise to an ability to forecast the weather. From this came the old sayings and beliefs that have been handed down from one generation to the next. There are still those who forecast the weather according to ancient traditions and natural signs.

TRADITIONAL HANDICRAFTS

Customs related to weddings have been important in upholding old traditions in handicrafts and folk art. Young girls made the textiles, linen and dresses for their own trousseaus, stored in a beautifully decorated and painted trunk. These she would show to a prospective suitor as proof of her skills and abilities.

The bridegroom, too, made presents for his bride. The most popular, especially in the western areas, were beautifully and intricately carved wooden objects like distaffs, mangle rollers, and different kinds of boxes and trunks. Old handicraft traditions have proved most resilient and have recently undergone a revival.

Finnish handicrafts first won international recognition when a *ryijy* rug was sent to the Swedish court in the 16th century. This was of the natural dyed, napped-type known in Scandinavia since the Bronze Age, and used as a cover with the nap side downwards. In 1900, the Flame *ryijy* designed by Akseli Gallen-Kallela won a gold medal at the Paris World Fair, and since the 1950s modern Finnish *ryijy* rugs have received increasing international recognition.

Handicraft traditions also include the making of a wide range of national costumes. The varieties and colours can be traced back to prehistoric times. It is now quite fashionable to wear a selfmade national costume to parties.

SAMI CULTURE

The Samis are the people living in the far north of Fennoscandia, and the oldest known inhabitants of that area. Their language, *Sami*, belongs to the Fenno-Ugrian family, and Sami culture is based on a pastoral way of life. To preserve and advance Sami culture and language, the Nordic countries set up the Nordic Sami Institute in 1973.

For the Samis the reindeer is a multi-purpose beast: it draws their sledges, carries their goods, provides meat and milk, and skins for clothes and tents. The Sami people are expert hunters and fishers. Their traditional dwelling is the transportable *kota*, a pole frame covered with skins, and insulated in winter with woven wool rugs. The numerous Sami national costumes, rarely seen these days, are extremely colourful affairs. Furs are extensively used in winter for coats, leggings and mittens.

The culture of the Orthodox Skolt Lapps, who moved from the Kola Peninsula and Petsamo areas during the last war, is quite different from that of the other Sami people.

LITERATURE

The oldest Finnish literature consists of the epic poems, folk legends and stories, and proverbs handed down by oral tradition. The written language was created by Mikael Agricola (1510–1557), who translated the New Testament, part of the Old Testament, and wrote the first Finnish ABC. Until the early 19th century, most works in Finnish were of a religious or popular educational nature, fiction being written in Swedish. Afterwards a deliberate movement to promote a Finnish culture and literature got underway. This was led by the statesman and philosopher J.V. Snellman (1806–1881) and the folklorist Elias Lönnrot (1802–1884). The Finnish Literature Society (established 1831) awarded Lönnrot a travel scholarship to enable him to continue collecting folklore. In 1835 the Society published his collection of epic folk poetry *Kalevala*, which was to become the very foundation of Finnish culture. In creating this great saga out of the oral runes he had collected, Lönnrot provided the nation with both a history and a literature. The *Kalevala* has been translated into almost 40 languages and is beyond doubt the best-known work of Finnish literature abroad.

With his *Tales of the Ensign Stål*, J.L. Runeberg (1804–1877) considerably influenced the rise of Finnish self-esteem and national identity; the poem "Our Land" in the book providing the words for the national anthem.

Although best known for his fairy tales, Zacharias Topelius (1818–1898) played an important role in awakening a sense of patriotism and history, and writing textbooks that were long used in the schools.

The period of Late Romanticism (1860–1880) produced Finland's most important author, Aleksis Kivi (1834–1872), the founder of modern Finnish literature. His epic romance *Seitsemän veljestä*, Seven Brothers, (1870) (translated into over 20 languages) and his plays are unsurpassed masters of prose and drama. His *Nummisuutarit*, The Village Cobblers, remains the finest comedy in the Finnish language.

The Realism of the 1880s embraces Minna Canth's (1844–1897) stark exposures of the injustices suffered by the working class and women, Juhani Aho's (1861–1921) portrayals of nature and ordinary folk, and Teuvo Pakkala's (1862–1925) descriptions of the life of the poor and children in small towns.

Karelianism, the dominant force at the turn of the century, drew its inspiration from the untouched wildernesses and rune lands of Karelia. The period exerted a considerable influence on the poet Eino Leino (1878–1926), clearly recognisable in the lines of his *Whitsongs*. The leading narrative writers of the first decade of the present century were Johannes Linnankoski (1869–1913), Ilmari Kianto (1874–1970), Joel Lehtonen (1881–1931) and F.E. Sillanpää (1888–1964). Sillanpää, whose works are imbued with a sympathetic and optimistic view of the world, received the Nobel Prize for literature in 1939. His major works are *Meek Heritage* (1919) and *The Maid Silja* (1931). Maria Jotuni (1880–1943) was one of the leading writers of plays and short stories at that time. Swedish-language literature, especially poetry, experienced a major breakthrough in the lyrics of Edith Södergran (1892–1923), the pioneer of modernism in Finland.

In more recent times, Mika Waltari (1908–1979) achieved

THE GREATEST NAMES IN FINNISH LITERATURE

Mikael Agricola (1510–1557)

Elias Lönnrot
(1802–1884)

J.L. Runeberg
(1804–1877)

Aleksis Kivi
(1834–1872)

Edith Södergran
(1882–1923)

Eino Leino
(1878–1926)

F.E. Sillanpää
(1888–1964)

Mika Waltari
(1908–1979)

Väinö Linna
(1920–1992)

Eeva-Liisa Manner
(1921–95)

Pentti Saarikoski
(1937–1983)

Paavo Haavikko
(1931–)

Bo Carpelan
(1926–)

international success. His great historical novels (like *The Egyptian*, which has also been filmed) have been translated into over 20 languages. Other significant novelists were Pentti Haanpää (1906–1955) with his portrayals of country people, nature and animals, and Toivo Pekkanen (1902–1957) for his descriptions of life in industrial society.

The Winter and Continuation Wars, territorial concessions, and the transformation of the country's internal and foreign situation, caused much self-searching and re-evaluation among writers. The leading representative of this new trend is Väinö Linna (1920–1992), whose novel *The Unknown Soldier* (1954) dealt with war in a refreshingly new and honest way through the eyes of an ordinary soldier. The book, which has sold over 600 000 copies and been adapted twice for the cinema, has been an unprecedented success. Linna's triology *Täällä Pohjantähden alla* (Here under the Northern Star) (1959–1962) is a socio-historical novel of a Finnish community over the past hundred years.

Veijo Meri (1928–) is one of the modernising forces in Finnish prose, and *The Manila Rope* (1957) is perhaps his best-known novel abroad. A close contemporary, Paavo Rintala (1930–), has combined a traditional with a more modern approach in his description of war. Eeva Joenpelto's (1921–) most important work is her Lohja series, a portrayal of the lives of a group of people between the wars. She won the Finlandia prize in 1994.

The leading figures in post-war literature in Swedish are Tito Colliander (1904–1989), Christer Kihlman (1930–), Henrik Tikkanen (1924–1984), the 1986 Finlandia Prize winner Jörn Donner (1933–), and Göran Schildt (1917–), the travel writer and biographer of Alvar Aalto. The Moomin family books of Tove Jansson (1914–), translated into almost 30 languages, have delighted children in all corners of the world.

Mainstream prose in the 1960s and 1970s was concerned with life among workers, the middle-class and the modernising countryside. The naturalistic, left-wing writer Hannu Salama (1936–) has produced the most vivid portrayals of the working-class milieu. Others writing in the same vein are Alpo Ruuth (1943–) and Lasse Sinkkonen (1937–1976).

Swedish-language prose has long concerned itself with the crisis of middle-class life, as the works of Kihlman and Tikkanen show. The same theme has been dealt with in Finnish by Kerttu-Kaarina Suosalmi (1921–), Anu Kaipainen (1933–) and Eeva Kilpi (1928–). In his novels and short stories, Antti Tuuri (1944–) uses industrialists and engineers to

"And what do you think happened then?" Tove Jansson's beloved Moomin and Little My picking berries in summertime with Moomin Mother.

convey his view of the world and social change. Other novels, several of which have been filmed, have been about war and emigration.

With increasing internationalisation and urbanisation, readers have turned to descriptions of country life, to the works of Kalle Päätalo (1919–). In his series of autobiographical novels he paints a detailed picture of the transformation of rural life. Eino Säisä (1935–1988) dealt with the same theme in his own series of novels. So different and unique were the writings of Timo K. Mukka (1944–1973) that it is difficult to categorise them. The setting for his greatest novel, *Maa on syntinen laulu* (The Earth is a Sinful Song), is the North, the theme is love, religion and death. This was made into a highly successful film that even won international recognition. The satirist Erno Paasilinna (1935–) won the first Finlandia Prize in 1985 for a collection of essays. The poet Nils-Aslak Valkeapää (1943–) has pioneered the culture of his own people, the Samis.

The radical transformation of poetry in the 1950s was spearheaded by the works of Aila Meriluoto (1924–) and Lauri Viita (1916–1965). Other representatives of the new poetry include Helvi Juvonen (1919–1959), the critic Tuomas Anhava (1927–), Eeva-Liisa Manner (1921–95), Eila Kivikk'aho (1921–) and Helvi Hämäläinen (1907–).

Paavo Haavikko (1931–), author, member of the Academy of Finland and publisher, is probably the most original poet of his generation. His widely translated *Selected Poems* include such brilliance that one can justifiably call him a genius. Haavikko is also a master of the novel, play, aphorism and historical essay. In 1984 he was awarded the much coveted Neustadt Prize for Literature.

Pentti Saarikoski (1937–1983) was often called the *enfant terrible* of Finnish literature. With his *Mitä tapahtuu todella?* (What happens really?) in 1962 he began a new chapter in political poetry. Saarikoski was also a gifted translator, skillfully rendering into Finnish the Greek and Latin classics, as well as modern writers like Joyce and Sallinger. His extensive knowledge was also reflected in his poetry, considered to be among the best ever written in Finland. The works of Saarikoski and other poets have been translated into English by Anselm Hollo (1934–), a poet himself who mainly writes in English. Other notable modern poets are Sirkka Turkka (1939–) and Arto Melleri (1956–), both Finlandia-prize winners.

It is worth while mentioning that each year Finnish publishers bring out a considerable number of firsts by hitherto unknown poets, which is one indication of the high regard poetry has in Finnish literature.

Among the best post-war Finnish-Swedish poets are Solveig von Schoultz (1907–), the author Bo Carpelan (1926–), Lars Huldén (1926–), the modernist, psychiatrist and Minister of Culture Claes Andersson (1937–), Finlandia-prize winner Gösta

Tampere City Library, designed by Raili and Reima Pietilä, and completed in 1986. It has the shape of the capercaillie bird it is named after.

Ågren (1936–) and the versatile Märta Tikkanen (1935–), who has received international recognition for her woman's interpretation of the world.

Writers in Finland are supported by the state through a system of grants, some of them for a number of years. Of the many prizes for literature, the Finlandia, awarded separately for fiction and non-fiction, is the biggest: both are worth FIM 100 000.

Finnish publishing houses are very active. About half of all books published are translations, mainly from English. Translated books account for about a half of the total, and most of them are from English.

LIBRARIES

As Finns are among the most avid readers in the world, it is fortunate that they have a widespread network of libraries. Public libraries are municipally owned but, like the scientific libraries, they are sub-sidised by the state. Readers are served by a network of 1025 branch libraries and an extensive fleet of bookmobiles. There are 800 scientific libraries and information centres in the country. Statistics for 1993 show that Finland holds almost all the world records related to public libraries. In proportion to its population, it has the highest number of registered borrowers, the highest borrowing rate, and one of the highest visiting rates.

At present the public libraries have 36.6 million books, 2.5 million recordings, videos and CD-ROMs. The scientific libraries have over 18 million volumes. These services are open to everyone, including resident foreigners.

The average borrowing rate from the public libraries is 19,7 books or recordings a year, making a total by 1993 of 99 million. The figure for scientific library borrowings is 4,5 million. Libraries also arrange literary evenings and children's events, operate an inter-lending service, and are developing an information retrieval service network.

Finland has for long been a pioneer in library building, and the two new central libraries completed in Helsinki and Tampere in 1986 have continued this tradition. Designed by Kaarlo Leppänen and Raili and Reima Pietilä respectively, they are both architecturally and functionally exceptional.

MUSIC

Finnish folk music has a long and rich tradition, which is kept alive through such annual festivals as that at Kaustinen. Finnish composers, too, have drawn their inspiration from folk music. The country's musical life, though diverse and vigorous, is, however, comparatively new. Nevertheless, performers and composers have given it a worthy reputation abroad.

Not until the end of the 18th century were there Finnish composers known by name. In the following century the leading figure was Fredrik Pacius. He organised the first orchestra and choir in Helsinki, wrote a number of operas, and set the national anthem "Our Land" to music. Jean Sibelius (1865–1957), already a foremost composer by the end of the 19th century, became a major symphonist in the early decades of this century. His extensive output includes seven symphonies, symphonic poems and orchestral suites inspired by ancient Finnish themes, an opera and a number of elegant minor works. Erik Tawaststjerna was the leading authority in the world on Sibelius, and his biography of the master has been translated into English.

Although many of the Finnish composers of this period worked in the shadow of Sibelius, they still managed to make a significant contribution to the country's music. Among them are Erkki Melartin, a productive writer of minature compositions, Toivo Kuula, whose tragic early death cut short a career as a composer

The young Jean Sibelius, Eero Järnefelt's portrait from 1894.

Aino Ackté was an opera singer of international repute at the beginning of the century. Albert Edelfelt's painting from 1901.

of songs for choir and solo voice, Selim Palmgren, the composer of piano and male choir music, the symphonist and opera composer Leevi Madetoja and the modernist Aarre Merikanto.

The symphonic poems of Uuno Klami resound with nationalist and impressionistic overtones. Yrjö Kilpinen is one of the greatest lied composers of the century.

In more recent times Erik Bergman has breathed new life into Finnish choral music and received international recognition for his vocal works. Einar Englund is well-known for his symphonies

The soprano Karita Mattila has sung in many famous opera houses in the world. This picture was taken after a performance of *Don Giovanni* at the New York Metropolitan.

and piano concertos, and the versatile Einojuhani Rautavaara has won many international prizes with his compositions. Bengt Johansson, Finland's first composer of electronic music, inspired others to follow in this field. Among the leading lights of the younger generation are the symphonist and opera composer Paavo Heininen, the composer and scholar Erkki Salmenhaara, the symphonist and concerto composer Pehr Henrik Nordgren, composer and conductor Esa-Pekka Salonen and the gifted symphonist Kalevi Aho. Composers of computer music include Kaija Saariaho, Jukka Tiensuu and Magnus Lindberg.

Finnish opera underwent a renaissance in the seventies and eighties with the appearance of Joonas Kokkonen's *The Last*

The Savonlinna Opera Festival is one of the main cultural events of the summer. The picture is from Aulis Sallinen's opera *The King Goes Forth to France*.

Temptations, Aulis Sallinen's *The Red Line* and *The Horseman*, and Paavo Heininen's *The Silk Drum* and *The Knife*. Opera has reached an ever widening section of the public through internationally important festivals at Savonlinna and Ilmajoki. Finnish opera has enjoyed an unprecedented success on the leading opera stages of the world like London and New York. World fame has come to many individual opera singers, starting at the beginning of the century with Aino Ackté, the soprano and founder of the Savonlinna Opera Festival, to the basses Matti Talvela, Jaakko Ryhänen and Matti Salminen, the basritone Jorma Hynninen, the sopranos Anita Välkki, Taru Valjakka and Karita Mattila as well as mezzo-soprano Monica Groop. Finns are enthusiastic operagoers. After the Finnish National Opera's new building opened in 1993, 96 % of performances during its first year were sold out.

Instrumentalists of national, and even international importance, include the pianists Ralf Gothóni, Eero Heinonen and Erik T. Tawaststjerna, and the cellist Arto Noras. The leading conductors include Paavo Berglund, Ulf Söderblom, Jorma Panula, Leif Segerstam, Okko Kamu, Esa-Pekka Salonen, Jukka-Pekka Saraste and Osmo Vänskä.

Jazz came to Finland fairly late, but thanks to the increase in foreign contacts, its position has gradually strengthened. Among the many musicians known abroad are saxophonist Eero Koivistoinen, guitarists Jukka Tolonen and Pekka Pohjala, trumpeter Simo Salminen, drummer Jukka-Pekka Uotila, composers and pianists Heikki Sarmanto and Jukka Linkola, and double-bass player Teppo Hauta-aho, and clarinetist and saxophonist Antti Sarpila.

The main jazz event of the year, the Pori Jazz Festival, is important enough to attract top international performers like Lionel Hampton, Oscar Peterson and Miles Davis.

Light music, whether played live by dance bands or on the radio and TV, continues to retain its great popularity. The most productive light music composer was Toivo Kärki, whose career extended over many decades. In the golden twenties comic songs were all the vogue; Alfred Tanner was the leading performer and Dallapé the best known dance band. Since then there have been many popular singers like Georg Malmstén, Tapio Rautavaara, Olavi Virta, Mauno Kuusisto, Marion Rung, M.A. Numminen, Hector, Tapani Kansa, Danny, Katri-Helena, Anneli Saaristo and Arja Saionmaa. The top rock musicians have been Tuomari Nurmio and Juice Leskinen, and the top groups Broadcast, Hurriganes, Sielun Veljet, Eppu Normaali and Lapinlahden Linnut, few of whom even earned a reputation abroad. One such was Hanoi Rocks, which broke up a few years back, and another the Havana Blacks. The Leningrad Cowboys, with their distinctive peaked hair styles and long pointed shoes, are extremely popular at the moment.

DANCE

In 1922 Edvard Fazer set up the Finnish National Ballet as part of the Finnish National Opera founded eleven years earlier. For the company's premiere, ballet masters George Gé and Alexander Saxelin produced

Finnish National Ballet dancers Kirsi and Jukka Aromaa have won many prizes in international ballet competitions.

Swan Lake in the spirit of Russian classical ballet.

The Finnish National Ballet also performed Swan Lake as its premier in the new opera house in 1993, this time under the direction of Vladimir Bourmeister, the Paris Opéra's ballet master. There are 64 permanent dancers

Maija Lavonen's "Path" ryijy rug.

Tapio Wirkkala's "Trunk" vase.

in the company, the majority of them Finns. The repertoire consists of both classic ballets and modern works by leading choreographers from the world of dance. The Helsinki City Theatre also has its own dance group, and there are several other smaller ones in the provinces.

The director of the Finnish National Ballet since 1992 has been Jorma Uotinen, a versatile and gifted dancer and choreographer, and a familiar visitor on many foreign stages.

Jorma Uotinen is considered to have revolutionised Finnish dance. He began with the National Ballet, transferred to modern ballet and was for many years a member of Carolyn Carlson's GRCOP dance group. From 1982 to 1991, he was artistic director of the Helsinki City Theatre. Today he is the best-known Finnish choreographer abroad. He has successfully danced and presented his own works in many European countries.

The leading dancers at the moment are Nina Hyvärinen, Anu Sistonen, Kirsi Aromaa, Minna Tervamäki, Sampo Kivelä and Timo Kokkonen

The international reputation of Finnish dance has been much helped by the annual Kuopio Dance and Music Festival, the only one of its kind in Scandinavia. This is one of the most exciting of Finland Festivals summer events.

DESIGN

The unique element in Finnish design is its closeness to nature. Nature has provided the motifs, shapes, colours, materials, and even influenced the treatment of materials.

Water is an essential part of Finnish nature, and the curving shores of lakes have inspired many works of art, like Alvar Aalto's famous Savoy vase. The play of light and colour in the changing seasons is reflected in the textiles, ryijy and raanu rugs of Irma Kukkasjärvi, Uhra Simberg-Ehrström, Elsa Montell-Saanio and Maija Lavonen, some ablaze with colours, others subtle and calm. Glass designers retain a predilection for flora and fauna motifs. Wood, however, remains the most popular material. The deep affection Finns have for the forests helps designers working by hand to express and accentuate its natural characteristics.

In the works of ceramic artists like Birger Kaipainen and Rut Bryk there is a clear Byzantine presence, although later on Bryk has become distinctly modernist.

When the teaching of design first began in the last century, one of the inspirations was national identity. Finnish design made its international debut at the Paris World Exhibition in 1900. In 1951 the American journal *House Beautiful* thought Tapio Wirkkala's wooden vase the most beautiful object in the

Steel fondue set and plastic containers designed by Timo Sarpaneva.

world, and a few years later Timo Sarpaneva's glass sculpture was awarded the same honour.

Quality design is timeless. The furniture designed by Alvar Aalto between the wars, and the works of many other designers from the fifties are still in production, selling well, and still as modern looking.

The fifties was the era of the star designers producing their one-off's or small runs. Nowadays, the emphasis is more on utility articles within the reach of all. The highly original yet practical design concept behind Marimekko's frocks and textiles ensured instant success at home and abroad. Vuokko Nurmesniemi, who started with Marimekko, went on to found her own company, producing similar, even more elegant dresses and textiles. Kaj Frank began in the fifties designing faience tableware, then moved on to other materials, even plastics. Heikki Orvola has created some fine and functional enamel kitchenware, as well as sculpturing in glass, and Oiva Toikka both utility and art objects in glass. Tapio Wirkkala was one of the greatest and most versatile designers this country has ever produced, equally at home with glass, metal, wood and porcelain. Timo Sarpeneva produces some artistic yet practical glass objects, nowadays very highly valued, and also utility articles in porcelain, cast iron, steel and plastic, and has even designed clothes and some exquisite silver objects. The silversmith Bertel Gardberg revolutionised metalworking in Finland, producing beautiful and simple cutlery in silver and steel. Antti Nurmesniemi and Yrjö Kukkapuro are the top names in interior design. Both they and Simo Heikkilä have a fine reputation as furniture designers. Pirkko Stenros is known for her safe and practical furniture for children and Stefan Lindfors has made a name for himself as a furniture and lamp designer.

In the world of fashion, the top designers today are Markku Piri in textiles, Isa Kukkapuro in clothes, Pertti Palmroth in footwear, Björn Weckström in jewellery, and Tua Rahikainen in furs.

The considerable achievements of Finnish industry would not be possible today without the know-how and artistic talents of the professional designers they employ.

THEATRE

The great popularity of the dramatic arts in Finland has its origins in old folk customs. Ancient rites to do with fishing and hunting, especially of bears, were carried over into wedding celebrations. Christianity, however, destroyed these old pagan customs, the church using dramatics for its own purposes and even taking it into the schools. The first theatrical performances in Finnish were in Turku in the 1650s, and the first theatres were built in the 19th century. Pietari Hannikainen's *Silmänkääntäjät* (The Conjurers), first performed in 1847, was the first play written in Finnish. The true beginning of Finnish-language theatre is, however, Aleksis Kivi's *Lea*, which had its first night in Helsinki in 1869. The National Theatre was founded in 1872. In addition to the professional theatre, Finland also has an extremely active amateur theatrical movement.

There are over 40 professional theatres in the country, and a considerable number of semi-professional and amateur theatres, summer theatres,

Wäinö Aaltonen's statue of the writer Aleksis Kivi occupies a place of honour outside the Finnish National Theatre.

student and youth groups. In terms of the number of theatres and the size of audiences, Finland is one of the leading countries in Europe. Frequent exchange visits are made between Finnish and foreign theatres. Of the many gifted directors, Vivica Bandler, Lasse Pöysti, Ralf Långbacka, Jack Witikka and Kalle Holmberg are perhaps the best known in Scandinavia. Undoubtedly the most gifted and controversial figure in modern Finnish theatre is Jouko Turkka, who is both a director and teacher. The leading school is the Academy of Dramatic Art in Helsinki, which also has a Swedish-language department.

Radio plays continue to fulfil an important role, as do the television theatres of the state and commercial networks.

Both Finnish and foreign plays are included in the extensive repertoires. An overview of the dramatic arts is provided each year by the well-attended Tampere Theatre Festival.

Since Finland became a member of the International Theatre Institute in 1950 its international ties have grown enormously.

CINEMA

Regular film production began in Finland in 1906, and the first talkie was made in 1931. Output fell off sharply with the arrival of television, partly due to excessive production in earlier years, but also to changed leisure habits. In recent years, about ten feature films have been produced annually. Film production is supported by the Finnish Film Foundation funded by the Ministry of Education.

Among the few internationally-known film directors are Jörn Donner, whose versatile production includes a documentary on Ingmar Bergman, and Rauni Mollberg, whose *Maa on syntinen laulu* (The Earth is a Sinful Song)

Both French and Finnish actors appeared in The Bohemians directed by Aki Kaurismäki.

Helsinki railway station, built between 1904 and 1919, is perhaps Eliel Saarinen's most famous building. On both sides of the main entrance are Emil Wikström's impressive "Torch Bearers".

has been successfully shown abroad. The Kaurismäki brothers, Aki and Mika, have almost become cult figures in Europe and the USA, their latest films even being made abroad. The most popular Finnish film of all time is Edvin Laine's adaptation of Väinö Linna's novel *Tuntematon sotilas* (The Unknown Solider), a new version of which was made by Mollberg in 1985. other important directors are the Pirjo Honkasalo and Pekka Lehto group, Anssi Mänttäri, Pekka Parikka, Heikki Partanen, Markku Pölönen and Markku Lehmuskallio. Renny Harlin, who was never a success in Finland, made a career for himself as a Hollywood producer and director.

ARCHITECTURE

Finland's oldest architectural monuments are its medieval stone castles and churches, and intricately carved, vernacular wooden churches and bell-towers from the 18th century. The greatest name in the early 19th century was C.L. Engel (1778–1840), who created the magnificent, uniform Neo-Classical centre of Helsinki.

National Romanticism, the dominant style at the turn of the century, contained influences from Karelian wooden architecture, medieval stone building, and the rich ornamentation of European Jugend Stil or Art Nouveau. The leading architects of the period were Eliel Saarinen (1873–1950), Herman Gesellius

(1874–1916), Armas Lindgren (1874–1929) and Lars Sonck (1870–1956). They designed both private houses and important public buildings, like the Helsinki Railway Station by Eliel Saarinen. This was probably his greatest work before leaving for the United States in 1923 to enrich its architecture. The twenties were dominated by the more severe lines of classicism and a struggle for a more rational style, the most monumental expression of which is J.S. Sirén's (1889–1961) Parliament building.

The breakthrough of functionalism came at the end of the 1920s with the works of Erik Bryggman (1891–1955) and Alvar Aalto (1898–1976), the greatest name in modern Finnish architecture. Internationally, Aalto is recognised as one of the great modernisers of architecture, whose influence is felt in urban and regional planning, interior and industrial design.

After the post-functionalism of Viljo Revell, Heikki Siren and Aulis Blomstedt, Alvar Aalto's individualistic white period and Reima Pietilä's unique expressionism, the seventies turned to constructivism, which stressed the social role of architecture. The urgent need for housing was met through serial production and prefabrication. In practice this often meant that a good idea became abominable architecture; only a few schemes, such as the Olari suburb by Simo Järvinen and Eero Valjakka, could be considered successful.

The 1980s saw the return to good architecture, in which the emphasis has been on humanism and environmental harmony, recalling the very best ideas of the now classic Tapiola Garden City from the 1950s. The timelessness of architecture has been accentuated in the restoration of old buildings and historic milieus, of which Katajanokka in Helsinki is perhaps one of the finest examples. Oulunsalo Town Hall, designed by the NVV office, is a good example of the new regionalism in architecture.

Reima (1923–93) and Raili Pietilä's, projects include the Finnish Embassy in New Delhi, Tampere City Library, and the president's official residence. Among the leading Finnish architects today are Kristian Gullichsen, Pekka Helin, Juha

Mikko Heikkinen and Markku Komonen have received much praise for their design for the Finnish embassy in Washington. The photo is of the entrance hall of the embassy.

Designs by Reima and Raili Pietilä often reflect the contours of the Finnish landscape, as in Mäntyniemi, the presidential residence.

Leiviskä and Juhani Pallasmaa.

Finnish architects continue to do well in invited competitions abroad, and have made a major contribution to export projects as these often require everything from design to construction.

PAINTING

The oldest examples of art in Finland are the numerous Stone Age rock engravings of Arctic hunting culture, and medieval frescoes in the stone churches of Åland, Lohja and Hattula, and the wooden churches of Ostrobothnia.

It was only with the establishment of the Fine Arts Society of Finland in 1848 that Finnish art really came into existence. Folk poetry and the *Kalevala* provided the inspiration for the national themes of

R.W. Ekman (1808–1873). The three von Wright brothers, Magnus (1805–1868), Wilhelm (1810–1887) and Ferdinand (1822–1906), painting largely in the Biedermeier spirit, are best known for their meticulous studies of fauna, but even their landscapes are considered masterpieces. The Düsseldorf School is represented by the landscape artist Werner Holmberg (1830–1860).

The true flourishing of Finnish art came towards the end of the 19th century, a golden age in which the influences of French naturalism were mixed with homespun national-romanticism, synthetism and early Italian Renaissance forms. The leading names of the period are the history painter Albert Edelfelt (1854–1905), and Finland's most versatile artist Akseli Gallen-Kallela (1865–1931), who found his inspiration as much in the *Kalevala* as in the nature and people of the untouched wilderness. Eero Järnefelt (1863–1937) is known for his sophisticated depictions of

Albert Edelfelt's scene from the Club War, "The Burned Village", powerfully portrays the depth of human fear.

the common people and fine portraits. Pekka Halonen (1865–1933) painted both monumental studies of the people and elegant, decorative landscapes. Juha Rissanen (1873–1950) painted ordinary people with a forceful monumentalism and subtle humour.

The main representatives of symbolism were Magnus Enckell (1870–1925) and Hugo Simberg (1873–1917). In the early years of this century two groups were established. The Septem Group in 1912, which was led by Magnus Enckell and inspired by French Post-Impressionism. The central figure of the expressionist November Group formed in 1917 was Tyko Sallinen (1879–1955), considered the founder of modern, national art. Though painting in a totally different way from Sallinen, Helene Schjerfbeck (1862–1946) can also be considered an expressionist. Her later works in particular possess a highly individual restraint and inner power. The first naïvists were Sulho Sipilä (1895–1949) and Vilho Lampi (1898–1936). Otto Mäkilä (1904–1955) became the central figure in the surrealist movement when it appeared in the twenties, but later, like other surrealists, he became an abstractionist. The spiritual heir

Strong, joyful colours speak out in "Street Scene", Rafael Wardi's oil painting from 1988.

Many of Hannu Väisänen's themes are taken from literature, as here in "Orpheus Playing".

The sculptress Eila Hiltunen's main work, the 24-ton Sibelius monument.

to the November Group was the October Group, set up in 1933. It was inspired by Aimo Kanerva (1909–1991), who was best known for his powerfully expressive oil and watercolour landscapes and portraits. The October Group also includes Unto Koistinen (1917–1994), whose portraits and female studies possess an imaginative and expressive quality.

In recent decades Finnish art has followed the international "isms" without losing its specifically national character. The dark-toned Ostrobothnian landscapes and interiors of Veikko Vionoja (1909–) and the dominant greens in Olli Miettinen's (1899–1969) rural scenes possess a characteristically fresh Nordic touch. An early representative of concretism was Birger Carlstedt (1907–1975), but its greatest exponent was Sam Vanni (1908–1992), the central figure in the Prisma Group set up in the 1950s. Among the many abstract painters, special mention can be made of Per Stenius (1922–) and Anitra Lucander (1918–). The foremost surrealists of today are Alpo Jaakola (1929–) and Juhani Linnovaara (1934–); the Lapp artist Reidar Särestöniemi (1925–1981) can also be considered a surrealist. The main representa-tives of neo-realism in the 1960s and 1970s are Jaakko Sievänen (1932–), Esko Tirronen (1934–), Juhani Harri (1939–), and Kimmo Kaivanto (1932–), who is also known for his graphics and sculptures.

The most famous illustrator of children's books in Finland was Rudolf Koivu (1890–1946). Erkki Tanttu (1907–1985) became a legend with his illustrations of folk humour, Björn Landström (1917–) for his drawings of ships, and Kari Suomalainen (1920–) for his satirical political cartoons.

The graphic arts flourished again in the 1950s in the wake of the international recognition accorded to Finnish design. A whole new generation came into being, with people like Ernst Mether-Borgström (1907–) and Tuulikki Pietilä (1917–) providing a new and vital artistic expression. The leading graphic artists today, Pentti Kaskipuro (1930–), Pentti Lumikangas (1926–) and Juhana Blomstedt (1937–), are recognised for their highly individual styles.

SCULPTURE

Very few of the works of early Finnish sculptors have survived. The most valuable wooden sculptures in medieval Finnish churches actually come from Gotland, Germany and the Netherlands. The oldest known Finnish medieval sculptor was the Master of Lieto.

The early pioneers were Erik Cainberg (1771–1816), who first used *Kalevala* motifs, and Carl Eneas Sjöstrand (1828–1906), whose realistic works had an enduring influence on embryonic Finnish sculpture. The main works of the classicist Walter Runeberg (1838–1920) are the statue to J.L. Runeberg (1885) in Esplanade park, Helsinki, and to Alexander II (1894) in Senate Square, Helsinki. Johannes Takanen's (1848–1885) talented works, especially his female and child figures, possess a natural plasticity and charm. Robert Stigell (1852–1907) leaned towards realism and the baroque, and his best known work is The Shipwrecked (1898) on the Observatory Hill in Helsinki. Perhaps the most gifted and individual sculptor was Ville Vallgren (1855–1940), whose output includes both massive public works and graceful miniature figures from fired clay in the Art Nouveau spirit. His most beloved work is the Havis Amanda fountain (1908) in Helsinki's market square, whose audacious Frenchiness aroused such a storm when first unveiled.

Undoubtedly the leading name in modern Finnish sculpture was Wäinö Aaltonen (1894–1966). He worked in bronze, ceramics and marble, but more importantly in granite – the first to use this element since the ancient Egyptians. Depending on the material used one of two features characterise his works: either a powerful monumentalism or a masculine lyricism. His main works are the statue to Aleksis Kivi (1939) in the Railway Square, Helsinki, the four figures (1929) on Hämeensilta Bridge, Tampere, the statue to Paavo Nurmi (1924) outside the Olympic Stadium, and the classical figures (1938) in the chamber of the Parliament building. Aimo Tukiainen (1917–) is a sculptor of memorials and busts, at first figurative but later abstract. Numerous cemeteries are adorned with his war memorials, but his most notable work is the equestrian statue of Marshal Mannerheim (1960) in Helsinki.

The modern scene is dominated by a number of highly expressive sculptresses. Eila Hiltunen (1922–) displays her original and imaginative versatility in welded metal fountains in Tampere and

The sculptor Tapio Junno was "Artist of the Year" in 1987. The picture is of his "Moon Window".

Helsinki, and the Sibelius Monument (1967) in Helsinki. The aesthetic Laila Pullinen (1933–) works in a combination of bronze and stone, and achieved a world reputation with her technique of exploding copper and bronze.

Kain Tapper (1930–), working mainly in wood, is one of the central figures of the expressionist, abstractionist trend. Others working in wood include Mauno Hartman (1930–) producing jointed logs inspired by the *Kalevala*, Eeva Ryynänen (1915–) with her massive human and animal forms, Heikki Virolainen (1936–) for his painted oak figures, and Alpo Jaakola (1929–) for his primitive wood sculptures and his paintings. An important young sculptress is Rauni Liukko (1940–), whose works are committed and subjective, repeatedly using such themes as women weighed down by labour, or children incarcerated in a violent and restrictive society.

Other socially critical young sculptors include Ossi Somma (1926–), Kimmo Kaivanto (1932–) and Kimmo Pyykkö (1940–).

RADIO, TELEVISION AND THE PRESS

RADIO AND THE HISTORY OF BROADCASTING

Broadcasting began in Finland in 1923 when radio hams made their first transmissions. Suomen Yleisradio (Finnish Broadcasting Company), nowadays Oy Yleisradio Ab or YLE for short, was established in 1926 to produce and transmit radio programmes in Finnish and Swedish, the two official languages of the country.

The following year the Radio Act came into force to regulate broadcasting. Nowadays the regulating authority is vested in Yleisradio Oy, the Finnish Broadcasting Company. Radio and TV broadcasting comes under the Ministry of Transport and Communications.

By the mid-fifties over half a

In the early years of radio broadcasting the radio towers in Lahti were famous landmarks symbolising the growing importance of this new means of communication.

Finland has a dense network of magazine stalls, selling both Finnish and foreign publications.

million licences had been issued, and today most households have one or more sets. YLE broadcasts 24 hours a day on three national stations, Ylen Ykkönen, Radiomafia and Radio Suomi. Radio Suomi also broadcasts regional programmes. In addition, YLE operates two Swedish-language stations.

Although YLE does not possess a *de jure* monopoly, in practice it has controlled broadcasting since the end of the last war. Since the mid-eighties, however, numerous local stations have come into existence, several of which are commercial. By the end of 1994 there were 61 of them.

TELEVISION

Students at the Helsinki University of Technology started television transmission in Finland in 1955. Within a year Tesvisio in Helsinki and Tamvisio in Tampere had received operators' licences. To finance their operations, both companies sold advertising space. After trial transmissions in 1957, YLE began regular transmissions from January 1, 1958. In spring 1957 another commercial company was set up, MTV, which rented time from YLE's TV channel. In 1964 YLE bought out Tesvisio and Tamvisio, forming them into its second channel, TV 2.

In 1986 a new commercial company, Oy Kolmostelevisio Ab (TV 3), established by YLE, MTV and Nokia Oy, began transmitting. At first TV 3's programmes could only be viewed in south Finland, but the area has been gradually extended to the rest of the country. In 1990 TV 3 became an MTV subsidiary and in 1993 all MTV and TV 3 programmes were transferred to a third network called MTV 3. As YLE owns all transmission networks, MTV 3 rents one of them. TV 4, which transmits Swedish programmes, commenced operations in 1988. It can only be seen in south Finland and on the west coast. There are a number of local cable TV companies in Finland, the largest of which is PTV which operates in Helsinki and the larger towns.

YLE's channels TV 1 and TV 2, as well as MTV 3, can be viewed throughout the country. YLE transmits an average of 119 hours a week on its two channels, and over 50 per cent of the programmes are Finnish made. YLE transmits news, sports, films, features, educational and entertainment programmes, etc. The most popular of them are Finnish serials, entertainments, films and sports features. Almost every household has at least one TV, most of them colour. VCRs have also become quite common.

All of YLE's radio and TV operations are financed from the sale of TV licences and payments by MTV. MTV payments include rent for the use of the third TV network and so-called public services.

THE PRESS

Finland's first newspaper appeared in Turku in 1771, and about the same time the first magazines saw the light of day. When Finland became a Grand Duchy in 1809 there was only one regularly published newspaper, and it was not until after the 1820s that more appeared. At first, these were in Swedish because their subscribers were Swedish-speaking. The oldest newspaper still being published is the Turku Swedish-language *Åbo Underrättelser*, founded in 1824.

According to FIEJ figures for 1994, the total circulation of Finnish dailies (newspapers appearing 4-7 times a week) is, in proportion to the population, the third highest in the world. There are 56 newspapers with a combined circulation of 2.48 million, or 512 copies per 1000 inhabitants. Approximately 5 % of these are in Swedish. In addition, there are 170 newspapers appearing only 1-3 times a week. Most people place a subscription for their newspaper, which is then delivered to their homes, usually in the early hours of the morning. The two evening newspapers published are bought from news stands.

There are nine newspapers published in the capital. The largest is Helsingin Sanomat, read by some three quarters of those living in the Helsinki area and 16-48 % of the rest of the population depending on the area.

Newspapers can either be politically independent or the mouthpiece of some party, which many of them were to start with. They were often established and owned by political parties. The political affiliation of newspapers has, however, greatly declined, and these days most of them call themselves independents.

The exact number of magazines in Finland is impossible to estimate because, in addition to the regularly published ones, there is a long tradition of printing and distributing free opinion-forming publications. The Post Office reckons it delivers over 1100 magazines, the vast majority of them reviews, trade and professional journals.

CIRCULATION OF NEWSPAPERS AND MAGAZINES

Average circulation of leading newspapers, 1995

Helsingin Sanomat (national, independent)	469 794
Ilta-Sanomat (evening)	212 806
Aamulehti (independent)	129 806
Turun Sanomat (independent)	111 545
Maaseudun Tuelvaisuus (independent)	103 645
Iltalehti (evening)	102 653
Kaleva (independent)	85 222
Keskisuomalainen (independent)	79 278
Kauppalehti (financal)	78 211
Savon Sanomat (independent)	72 283

Average circulation of leading magazines, 1995

Valitut Palat (Reader's Digest)	346 434
Aku Ankka (comic)	283 337
Seura (general interest)	265 919
Apu (general interest)	250 305
et-lehti (senior citizens)	229 606
Kotivinkki (women)	202 804
Kotiliesi (women)	202 516
Kodin Kuvalehti (women)	176 747
Anna (women)	147 964
7 päivää (general interest)	138 494

(Sources: Sanomalehtien liitto/Levikintarkastus Oy).

SPORT

THE MOST POPULAR SPORTS
For centuries Finns have been keen on subjecting themselves to trials of strength, speed and agility. The Royal Academy of Turku had an instructor in swordmanship immediately it was established in 1640, sports became part of military life from the 1780s onwards, and the schools and universities showed a similar interest in the early 19th century. The first sports clubs came into existence in the 1850s.

Whether as participants or spectators, Finns take a serious interest in sport. In wintertime, pre-school kids and senior citizens alike go in for cross-country skiing. Slalom is increasing in popularity, especially among young people. Every weekend mass long-distance skiing events are organised, the greatest of which is the 75 km Finlandia Skiing Marathon from Hämeenlinna to Lahti in which over 10 000 enthusiasts participate. When summer comes the Finns start jogging, swimming, cycling, playing football and *pesäpallo*, the Finnish version of baseball. Orienteering is also very popular. As the country has a great number of swimming halls, people can swim throughout the winter. The games that draw the most spectators are ice hockey, football, athletics and skiing. Trotting, car and motorbike racing, rally driving, ball games, golf and so on, are all quite popular and have no lack of participants or spectators.

GREAT FINNISH VICTORIES
Finland first entered the Olympics at the intermediate games in Athens in 1906 where it also scored its first victory: Verner Weckman in wrestling. The country was still a Russian Grand Duchy when it took part in the Stockholm Olympics in 1912, this time winning 9 gold medals. The hero was the long-distance runner Hannes Kolehmainen, who won the 5000 m, 10 000 m and marathon and of whom it is said that he "ran Finland on to the map of the world". Between 1906 and 1994, Finland has won 416 Olympic gold medals, 123 of them in Winter Olympics.

Athletics appear to be a Finnish strong point, especially long-distance running and javelin. The most famous Finnish runner was Paavo Nurmi who, in the Olympics between 1920 and 1928 won 9 gold and 3 silver medals. During his career he set 31 outdoor track world records. Almost in the same class was Nurmi's fellow runner Ville Ritola, who won five gold medals. The top runner in more recent times is

Many feel that the 1952 Helsinki Olympics were the last true games.

MONDIALI DI NUOTO ROMA

Jani Sievinen and Antti Kasvio are Finland's top swimmers.

Lasse Virén, who won the 5000 and 10 000 metre events in the 1972 and 1976 Olympics. In the javelin, Finns have three times walked off with triple victories.

In Olympic wrestling Finland was the leading country in the 1920s. It has also won medals in gymnastics, canoeing and many other events. The victories of oarsman Pertti Karppinen and canoeist Mikko Kolehmainen show that even such less traditional sports have gained in popularity.

In cross-country skiing Finns have won many gold medals in the Olympics and world championships. The finest skiers of the older generation were the men Veli Saarinen, Veikko Hakulinen and Eero Mäntyranta, and the women Helena Takalo and Hilkka Riihivuori. Marja-Liisa Kirvesniemi became a national hero when she won three golds and one bronze at the Sarajevo Winter Olympics in 1984.
A new star emerged at the 1988 Calgary Games, when Marjo Matikainen won a gold and two bronzes. Finns have also been successful as ski jumpers. In the 1980s, Olympic winner and world master Matti Nykänen was unbeatable. He won three golds at the Calgary Winter Olympics -

Jari Litmanen is a star player with Ajax, the Dutch football team.

Juha Kankkunen, world champion rally driver in 1986, 1987, 1991 and 1993.

something which nobody has ever done before, ie. win three times in the same games. In 1992, 16-year-old ski jumper Toni Nieminen won the world championship and two golds and one bronze in the Albertville Winter Olympics.

Ice hockey is so popular among youngsters that a special junior league has been set up. Several Finnish players, like Jari Kurri, Teemu Selänne and Saku Koivu, play for professional teams in the United States and Canada.

The Finn Jari Litmanen who plays in Ajax, scored top goals in 1993/94 and was elected best football player in the Dutch league in that season.

Motor sports is another field in which Finns have become world famous. The best known rally drivers today are Marrku Alen, Ari Vatanen, Juha Kankkunen, Timo Salonen and Hannu Mikkola, winners of many world events. Heikki Mikkola is the leading figure in motorcross racing, and Keke Rosberg was the first Formula One driver to come from Finland. He won the world championship in 1982 and, although he subsequently dropped out of racing, Keke is probably still the best-known Finnish sportsman in the world. Mika Häkkinen and Mika Salo are the current Formula-one drivers.

Although football is gaining in popularity, Finland is still streets away from becoming top of the European league. American football has also caught on, Finland even becoming one of the best in Europe. It is probably true to say that there is a club in Finland for every conceivable sport.

THE IMPORTANCE OF SPORT IN FINLAND

There are dozens of sports associations in Finland. Suomen liikunta ja urheilu ry, the Finnish Sports Federation, is the central organisation of Finnish sports associations. The total individual membership of the approximately 6000 associations is 1.1 million.

The main centres for instruction and research are the universities of Jyväskylä and Tampere, the UKK Institute (named after President Kekkonen), the research centre for competitive and top rank sports in Tampere and a number of sports institutes. Sport receives financial support from the proceeds of the state-owned Oy Veikkaus Ab which runs football pools, trotting races, national and other lotteries.

Top athletes normally receive training grants from their own associations, and Olympic Games' entrants from the Finnish Olympic Committee. International competition winners are much feted heroes, often being given houses financed by donations or public subscription. As it is not possible to be a professional in Finland, many league-grade ice hockey and football players join European or American teams.

Finland's tremendous enthusiasm for sport is proven by its interest in hosting such major events as the 1952 Olympic Games and the first World Athletics Championships in 1983, both in Helsinki, as well as world ice hockey and skiing championships.

THE FINNISH LIFESTYLE

Large families were quite normal in the old Finnish agrarian society, with several generations often living under the same roof. Even in the first half of this century it was still common that a son brought his bride home to live with his parents. As economic life diversified, more and more people changed over to the newer occupations and left to live in the towns and industrial centres. The large family disappeared, and nowadays it is very rare for grandparents to live with their children. The children have left to study or work elsewhere, leaving their parents to carry on in the home areas. When the time comes to go on pension, people often go to live in centres where they have acquired retirement flats, or to some senior citizen's centre especially designed to cater for their needs. There are also special homes for old people no longer capable of looking after themselves.

The mass migration of people from the countryside to the towns in the fifties and sixties caused an acute housing problem as it was almost impossible to find

The nutritional value of Finnish rye bread is very high. In olden days, when the bread was baked at home, it was kept on rods suspended from the ceiling.

rented accommodation because tenants were so protected in law that landlords had found more attractive ways of investing their wealth. These protective laws have now been repealed. People are, however, encouraged to buy their own homes, and it is nothing unusual for the first flat to be bought whilst still studying. Finns own approximately 400 000 summer cottages in addition to a flat or house. Even when students study in their home towns, they leave home to be free and independent.

Class distinctions in Finland have so narrowed that nowadays the difference is more in lifestyle than income. True poverty has virtually disappeared following the radical improvements in medical care, family allowances, unemployment benefits and pensions since the war. Although there are still income differences between occupations, basic necessities are guaranteed. There is now talk of the "new poor", people who have lived beyond their means and have sunk heavily into debt due to the availability of easy credit.

Differences between rural and urban lifestyles can be seen most clearly in consumption; what people spend their money on. In the larger cities the lifestyle is much the same as elsewhere in the world, and the effect of internationalisation on national culture is all too apparent. There are lesser opportunities for affluent living in the countryside.

Finns have a great respect for education, often considering it more important than income. Thus they respect the legal, medical and teaching professions, even though higher incomes could be earned elsewhere. For example, Finns rarely address each other as Mr or Mrs, but by professional titles such as Secretary or Director or their academic qualifications such as Doctor or Professor.

With rapid industrialisation in the sixties, more and more women joined the labour force. Nowadays the majority of mothers of pre-school children go to work. Although the law requires that all pre-school children should have a place in the municipal daycare centres, this has not been possible to arrange yet. Most pre-school children spend 8 to 9 hours a day in some form of day care. Six-year-old children are in pre-school groups and start proper school when they are seven. They can, however, start school at six if their parents so desire. Divorce, unfortunately, is on the increase as are single-parent units. It is also increasingly normal to form common-law marriages, which have the same status in law as conventional marriages. The average Finnish family has two children, and only very few have four or more children. This is partly because ever more women spend longer studying or prefer to establish their careers before starting a family. It is nothing unusual for the first child to be born when the mother is over thirty. Few families, even rich ones, have domestics, so child upbringing and household chores are divided, often unevenly, between the parents.

Most Finns enjoy a month's holiday in summer and a week in winter, the latter normally taken during the school skiing holiday in February. Some spend their summers at summer cottages in the peaceful countryside, often beside a lake, others travelling around the country, camping or visiting relatives. An increasing number of people prefer to spend part of their holidays abroad, on the sunny beaches of Spain, Greece or Italy, or even travelling to the exotic East.

Sport is undoubtedly the most popular pastime in Finland: cross-country skiing, slalom or ice hockey in the winter, and

Folk dancing is still very popular and courses well attended. The best time to see the dancers in their colourful national costumes is at Midsummer.

swimming, walking, jogging, cycling, fishing, sailing or even playing golf in the summer. Finland has all the water and untouched nature that could be desired. Finns are also avid readers, borrowing an average of 19,7 books a year from their local libraries. These are very important leisure-time centres, especially in the countryside. Adult education is also very popular, with even the smallest village running courses in anything from information technology to Spanish. Watching television is also popular. There is a theatre in every town and a strong amateur theatrical movement in the countryside.

Because the Finnish language is so different from Indo-European languages, Finns are somewhat hesitant to exercise their linguistic skills in conversation with foreigners. They are often thought to be shy, but once you get to know them they are just the same as other people. There are perhaps some differences – the people from Savo and Karelia are considered more jovial and sociable than those from Häme and the south-west. Finns also have a tendency towards melancholy, which perhaps explains why dreamy tangos are so popular in the restaurants where they go at the weekends to drink and dance. Drinking is also a problem for some, not that they drink too often, but too much at one time.

Although one cannot claim that Finns are religious, most of them are baptised and confirmed and prefer being married and buried by the church. Here, as elsewhere, the great Christian feasts of Christmas and Easter are very commercial, replete with traditional foods and the exchange of presents. These are old pagan customs which continue to thrive. The third great festival, Midsummer, is when the cities empty and the countryside is adorned with national costumes, flags and pennants. Mothers' Day is in May, Fathers' Day in November. Also every

Finns are dead keen on sports and like to take part in mass events. The greatest of these is the Finlandia Skiing Race, when more than 10 000 people ski the 75 km from Hämeenlinna to Lahti.

For most Finns the weekly sauna is still a must, and the best way to relax and forget about work.

day is a nameday, celebrated in offices and homes with coffee and cakes. As coffee is drunk on every possible social occasion, this has made Finns the world's largest coffee consumers. It is served on birthdays, namedays, engagement parties, reading the banns, weddings, funerals, graduations – the list is unend-

Forests are an essential part of nature, somewhere to pick berries and mushrooms, or just breathe fresh air and the resinous scent of the fir. The picture is of a typical birch glade.

ing. And not just coffee, but a vast array of buns, cakes, cookies and biscuits.

Whilst on the subject of these all-important Finnish rituals, one must not forget the sauna – and naturally the after-sauna coffee. In the countryside the whole family visits the sauna on Saturday evening, the sauna building normally ajoining the house or farm. In the towns apartment blocks usually have only one sauna for the tenants, so it is necessary to stagger visits throughout the week. The custom of visiting the sauna, however, has never been given up, and many newly built flats and houses in the towns now have their own sauna. Foreigners are always invited to have a sauna and beat out grime and tiredness with a fragrant bunch of leafy birch twigs. Finns are naturally proud that sauna is the one Finnish word that has spread throughout the world. The sauna is perhaps the oldest of all Finnish institutions. Its effect is not only cleansing, but relaxing and calming, and the feeling of well-being that comes with it is really worth experiencing. You can say no to almost anything else in Finland, but not to an invitation to a sauna. This is the only way in which a foreigner can ever get to grips with the true Finnish soul.

WHO'S WHO IN FINLAND

Aalto, Jorma S. (1935),
chancellor of Justice since 1986.
Doctor of Laws. Lecturer at the
universities of Helsinki and Turku since
1960, professor of procedural law since
1975. Parliamentary Ombudsman
1974–77, 1978–81 and 1982–86.

Ahtisaari, Martti (1937,)
president of the Republic, elementary
school teacher. Ambassador, eg. Dar es
Salaam 1973–77. Special representative
of the Secretary General of the United
Nations to Namibia 1978–90, Under-
Secretary of State for development
cooperation at the Ministry for Foreign
Affairs 1984–86. Assistant Under-
Secretary of the United Nations 1987–
91. Chairman of the United Nations
Bosnia-Herzegovina Working Group in
1992 and 1993. Secretary of State at the
Ministry for Foreign Affairs 1991–94.
President of the Republic since 1994.

Aho, Esko (1954),
politician, Master of Political Science.
Member of Parliament since 1983.
Held various positions in the Centre
Party, chairman since 1990. Prime
minister 1991–95.

Berglund, Paavo (1929),
conductor. First violinist of the Radio
Symphony Orchestra 1949–58,conductor
1955–62, senior conductor 1962–71.
Director of the Bournemouth Symphony
Orchestra 1972–79 and Helsinki Philharmonic Orchestra 1975–79, visiting chief
conductor of the National Orchestra of
Scotland (Glasgow) since 1981. Chief
conductor of the Stockholm Philharmonic
Orchestra 1987–91. Chief conductor of
the Royal Danish Orchestra since 1993.
Numerous recordings. Acclaimed for his
interpretations of Sibelius, Brahms and
Shostakovitch.

Bergman, Erik (1911),
composer, professor, member of
the Academy of Finland. Studies in
Finland, Central Europe and Italy, music
critic, choir director and professor at
Sibelius Academy 1963–76. Leading
Finnish composer and pioneer of a new
music free of national traditions. Untiring
search for new paths and for an independent, unconventional approach.
Winner of the international Sibelius prize
in 1965.

Carpelan, Bo (1926)
author, critic, Ph. D. Assistant chief
librarian at the City of Helsinki library
1964-80, artist professor 1980-93. Has
written poetry, novels, children's books
and literary studies. Of special merit are
his Axel, a semi-factual novel about Axel
Carpelan, the patron of Jean Sibelius,
and the Finlandia prize winning Urwind.
Has received four State prizes for
literature, Nordic Council Literature prize
1977, State Translator prize 1985,
Thanks for the Book prize 1988, and
Finlandia prize 1993.

Cantell, Kari (1932),
medical researcher, professor. Doctor of
Medicine and Surgery 1959, director of
the department of virology at the Institute of National Health. International
recognition for work on the use of
interferon in the treatment of cancer
and virus diseases.

Ehrnrooth, Casimir (1931)
chairman of the board, LL.M., mining
counsellor. Managing director of Oy
Kaukas Ab 1967-85, CEO of Kymi
Strömberg/Kymmene Oy 1986-91,
chairman of the board 1991-96. Vice-
chairman of the board of UPM-
Kymmene Corporation since 1996.
French honorary consul 1977-85.
Member of the boards of administration
of several companies. Member of the
European Round Table of Industries
since 1993.

Erkko, Aatos (1932),
newspaper publisher. Editor-in-chief of *Viikko-Sanomat* 1953–61 and *Helsingin Sanomat*, Finland's largest national daily, 1961–72, and managing director of their publishers Sanoma Oy, 1965–76, and chairman of the board since 1972.

Groop, Monica (1958)
opera mezzo-soprano, M.Mus. Sang with the Finnish National Opera 1989-91. Visiting opera, oratorio and lied singer throughout the world, known particularly as an interpreter of Baroque music. Cardiff song competition finalist 1989. Major success in the new interpretation of Pelléas and Mélisande in San Francisco 1995. Numerous recordings.

Gothóni, Ralf (1946),
pianist, professor. Teacher at Sibelius Academy 1968–69, 1970–73 and professor 1991. Pianist with Royal Opera of Stockholm 1969–70. Freelance performer since 1973. Professor Hamburg School of Music since 1987. Lectures and courses in Finland and abroad. Artistic director of Savonlinna Opera Festival 1984–87, artistic director of Finlandia Sinfonietta since 1989. Over 50 recordings, worked as conductor, composed works for voice and piano. Several awards and prizes, including the internationally esteemed Gilmore Art Award in 1994.

Haavikko, Paavo (1931),
author, publisher, honorary Doctor of Philosophy and a member of the Academy of Finland. One of the foremost modern Finnish writers, first Scandinavian to receive the coveted Neustadt prize for literature in 1984. Nine state prizes for literature. Has written poetry, aphorisms, radio and theatre plays, librettos, short stories, novels and essays. Poetry translated into many languages. Wrote the script for the TV film *The Age of Iron*, which won the Prix Italia in 1983. Member of the board of the Finnish Society of Authors since the early 1960s. Literary director of Otava Publishing Company 1967–83, managing director of Arthouse Publishing Company 1985.

Hägglund, Gustav (1938),
chief of Defense of the Finnish Defence Forces since 1994. General. Research professor at Harvard University 1981–82. Commander of the Finnish UN peacekeeping forces 1978–79, commander of the UNDOF peacekeeping forces in Golan 1985–86 and UNIFIL peacekeeping forces in South Lebanon 1986–88. Commander of the South-East Finland military area 1986–90. Chief of the General Headquarters 1990–94. Studies published in Finland and the United States.

Hämäläinen, Sirkka (1939),
governor of the Bank of Finland, D.Sc. (Econ.). Various positions in the Bank of Finland, acting head of economics department 1961–81, director 1982–91, member of the board 1991–92, governor since 1992. Also director general, economics department of the Ministry of Finance 1982–91.

Halonen, Tarja (1943)
minister for Foreign Affairs, LL.M., SAK (Central Organisation of the Finnish Trade Unions) lawyer 1970–79. Member of Parliament since 1979. Second Minister of Social Affairs and Health 1987–90, Minister of Justice 1990–91, Minister for Foreign Affairs since 1995.

Harlin, Renny (1959),
movie producer and director. Short film producer and director for advertizing bureaus and Finnish Broadcasting Company 1979–82. Productions and directions in Hollywood since 1983 include Arctic Heat, Prison Nightmare on Elm Street 4, Ford Fairlane, Die Hard 2, Rambling Rose and Cliffhanger. Awards for advertising and short films in Finland, international film festivals and two-time Oscar candidate.

Herlin, Pekka (1932),
board chairman, B. Sc. (Econ.). Career at Kone Corporation, administrative director 1958–62, deputy managing director 1962–64, managing director 1964–87, chairman of the board since 1987. Kone Corporation, which has subsidiaries and factories in several countries, produces lifts.

Hynninen, Jorma (1941),
opera singer, professor. School teacher 1964, studied music in Finland and abroad in late 1950s and early 1970s, soloist at the Finnish National Opera since 1970, and artistic director 1984–90. Artistic director of the Savonlinna Opera Festival 1991–. Professor at Sibelius Academy since 1996. Performed in operas and lied concerts in all major music centres. One of the leading baritones of our time. Leading opera roles include the Count of Almaviva in the *Marriage of Figaro*, Figaro in the *Barber of Seville*, Rodrigo in *Don Carlos*, and Topi in *The Red Line*.

Hiltunen, Eila (1922),
sculptress, professor. Numerous exhibitions abroad, including New York 1969 and Rome 1985, and others supported by Ministry for Foreign Affairs in Ottawa and Philadelphia in 1982. Works in several museums in Finland and abroad. Most famous work is the Sibelius Monument (1967) in Helsinki, studies for which are in Montreal and outside the UN building in New York. Eila Hiltunen's sculptures are usually large and impressive.

Ihalainen, Lauri (1947),
chairman of the Central Organisation of Finnish Trade Unions (SAK) since 1990. Previously occupied various positions in SAK, including youth secretary 1970–77, organisation secretary 1977–84, secretary 1984–90.

Ihamuotila, Jaakko (1939),
CEO, engineer. Assistant and later assistant professor in physics at the Helsinki University of Technology in 1960s, planning engineer with Imatran Voima Oy 1966–68, planning engineer, assistant director, planning director, managing director and vice chairman of the board of Valmet Oy 1968–79, CEO and chairman of the board of Neste Oy since 1980. Member of the boards of many companies and business organisations.

Jansson, Tove (1914),
authoress, artist, honorary Doctor of Philosophy (Åbo Academy). Art studies in Finland and abroad. Prizes in Finland and other countries. First book, *Moomin and the Comet*, published 1946. Since then tens of Moomin books have delighted children throughout the world. Translations into almost 30 languages. Several literary prizes, including H. C. Andersen medal, Austrian state prize, Swedish Academy prize, and Le Prix de l'Office Chrétien du Livre.

Jakobson, Max (1923),
managing director, diplomat, honorary Doctor of Political Science (Helsinki). Director for political affairs at the Ministry for Foreign Affairs in 1960s, Finland's permanent representative to the UN 1965–72, Finnish ambassador to Stockholm 1972–74, managing director of the Council of Economic Organisations of Finland (EVA) 1975–84. Published several works on recent Finnish history which have been translated into different languages.

Johannes
(Rinne, Johannes Wilho) (1923), archbishop of the Finnish Orthodox Church (Finland's second official church), Doctor of Theology. Assistant bishop 1969, bishop of Helsinki 1970, metropolitan of Helsinki 1972, archbishop since 1987, pro-term archbishop of Estonia since 1996.

Kahri, Tapani (1938),
deputy managing director of the Confederation of Finnish Industries and Employers (TT) since 1988. Director for labour market policy. Master of Laws. Various positions in TT since 1965, director 1971–79, managing director of the Finnish Employers' General Group 1980–88.

Kankkunen, Juha (1959),
rally car driver. World rally car champion 1986, 1987, 1991 and 1993, silver medal 1992 and bronze medal 1989 and 1990. Chosen Sportsman of the year in Finland in 1993.

Kamu, Okko (1946),
conductor. Studied the violin and played in several orchestras. Won the international Karajan competition for young conductors, Berlin, 1969. Has served as senior conductor of the Radio Symphony Orchestra 1972–77, Oslo Philharmonic Orchestra 1975–79, artistic director of the Helsinki Philharmonic Orchestra 1981–88. Several times visiting conductor abroad. Known for his great musical sensitivity and vitality, which comes into its own in a classical-romantic repertoire. Conductor of the Finnish National Ballet since 1996.

Kaurismäki, Mika (1955),
film producer and director. With his brother **Aki** (1957) represents the younger generation in the Finnish film industry. They have produced and directed films together and separately, in Finland and abroad, and which have achieved international success.

Koivisto, Mauno (1923),
president of the Republic 1982–94,
Doctor of Philosophy. Served in various
positions in banking since 1957,
chairman of the board of the Bank of
Finland 1968–82. Minister of Finance in
several governments, prime minister
1968–70 and 1979–82, represents the
Social Democratic Party. Assumed the
duties of president when President
Kekkonen fell sick in autumn 1981,
elected president in 1982 and again
in 1988.

Leiviskä, Juha (1936)
architect, artist professor. Own
architectural office 1967–77, in partnership with Vilhelm Helander since
1978. Major works include Kouvola
town hall (with Bertel Saarnio) 1964–68,
Myyrmäki church and parish centre
1980–84, German Embassy in Helsinki
(with Rosemarie Schnitzler–Mattila and
Nicholas Mayow), Hakushi restaurant
design, Japan and Smista Business
Centre, Huddinge, Sweden 1990–91.
Several first prizes in architectural
competitions, Carlsberg prize in 1995,
member of architectural competition
juries. Works often featured in domestic
and foreign professinal journals.

Kokkonen, Joonas (1921),
composer, member of the Academy
of Finland. Teacher at the Sibelius
Academy in the 1940s and 1950s,
and professor of composition 1959–63,
after which he was appointed to the
Academy of Finland. Successful
composer of operas and chamber
music, and as a symphonist has made a
highly original contribution to Finnish
music. Won the international Sibelius
prize in 1973. Main opera, *The Last
Temptations*, has been performed at
the New York Metropolitan.

Liikanen, Erkki (1950),
EU comissioner, politician, M.Sc.(Pol.).
Member of Parliament 1972–90.
Secretary of the Social Democratic Party
1981–87, Minister of Finance 1987–90.
Ambassador of Finland to the European
Community and later the European
Union 1990–94. EU comissioner since
1995.

Lindberg, Magnus (1958)
composer. One of the best known Finnish composers of modern music. His music is typified by a preference for theoretical structures, severe constructivity and a strict mastery over resources. His "Kraft", "Kinetics" and "Marca" have received special recognition, likewise "Aura". Winner of the UNESCO International Composer Rostrum 1982, 1986, Nordic Council Music prize 1987, Prix Italia 1986, Koussevitzky prize 1988, William Hansen prize 1988 and British Royal Philharmonic Society prize 1993.

Lipponen, Paavo (1941),
prime minister. Chairman of Finnish Social Democratic Party 1993–. Occupied several positions in the party since 1967. Member of Parliament 1983–87 and since 1991. Political secretary to Prime Minister 1979–82. City of Helsinki councillor 1993–95. Prime Minister 1995–.

Lindfors, Stefan (1962),
interior architect, furniture designer. Teacher at the University of Industrial Art, Helsinki University of Technology, Danish Design School and Oslo University of Industrial Art, professor at the Kansas City Art Institute since 1993. Stage settings, designs for lamps, furniture, store interiors, exhibitions, catalogues, advertising campaigns and packagings for Finnish and foreign companies. Sculptures in eg. Helsinki airport domestic terminal, works in Finnish museums and in Gothenburg. STO Interior Design Award 1993, Georg Jensen Prize 1992, Väinö Tanner Trailblazer Award 1992 and Finnish Foundation of Visual Arts Stipend 1992.

Mattila, Karita (1960),
opera soprano. Won the Lappeenranta (1981) and BBC Cardiff (1983) voice competitions. Successful performances in the Finnish National Opera and with opera companies in Paris, London, New York and Brussels, mainly singing Mozart operas.

Niemelä, Juha (1946)
president and CEO, M.Sc.(Econ.).
Marketing manager in various paper
companies. General manager,
Paperituote 1979-83, senior vice
president United Paper Mills Ltd, 1983-
93, executive vice president 1993-96,
president and CEO, UPM-Kymmene
Corporation since 1996.

Ollila, Jorma (1950)
CEO, M.Sc. (Econ.), M.Sc. (Eng.), M.Sc.
(Pol.). Various positions in Oy Nokia Ab,
deputy managing director international
operations 1985-86, deputy managing
director for finance 1986-89, managing
director Nokia Mobile Phones 1990-92,
since 1992 group CEO and chairman of
the board. On the boards of several
Finnish and foreign companies and
business organisations.

Niinistö, Sauli (1948)
politician, court of appeals justice, party
chairman. Worked in his own law office
and as a prosecutor in the Turku Court
of Appeals 1977-87. Member of
Parliament since 1987. Chairman of the
Constitutional Committee since 1987.
Occupies several positions of trust in the
town of Salo and the National Coalition
Party. Chairman of the National Coalition
Party since 1994. Minister of Justice
1995-96, Minister of Finance since 1996.

Pallasmaa, Juhani (1936),
architect, professor. Joint architectural
design work with various Finnish architects since 1962, own architectural
office since 1983. Professor of Architecture Helsinki University of Technology
since 1991, director of the Museum of
Finnish Architecture 1976–83, rector
University of Industrial Art 1972–74.
Major works include Finnish Institute in
Paris 1991, Helsinki East Centre shopping mall 1992. Has designed town
planning, industrial art and art exhibitions. Visiting professor of architecture
at foreign universities, editor of books
and exhibition catalogues, lectures and
articles. Honorary member of the
International Academy of Architecture
and Institute of American Architects.

Piri, Markku (1955)
textile designer, managing director, designer for Marimekko Oy 1979-81, designer and managing director of Markku Piri Inc since 1986. Teacher at the Parsons School of Design 1982. Has designed home fabric sets, clothes, footwear, household objects, furniture, gifts and graphics. Designer for Jorma Uotinen's Dance Theatre and the Cullberg Ballet since 1978. Artistic Director of the European Championship Games, Helsinki, 1994. Numerous exhibitions (also of paintings).

Rehn, Elisabeth (1935),
politician B.Sc. (Econ.). Active in business life and education. Member of Parliament 1979–. Chairman of the Parliamentary Group of the Swedish People´s Party 1987–90. Minister of Defence 1990–95. Candidate in the 1994 Presidential elections. UN Human Rights inspector in Bosnia-Herzegovina in 1996. Member of the boards of several foundations and companies.

Potila, Antti (1938),
company president, M. Sc. (Comm.). Various positions in Oy Strömberg Ab 1964–78, managing director 1979–83, CEO of Rauma-Repola Oy 1984–87, president of Finnair Oy since 1987. Served on the boards of several companies.

Saariaho, Kaija (1952),
composer. Studied composition in Germany. She worked in several electronic music studios, at present in IRCAM, the Institute of Acoustic Music at the Pompidou Centre, Paris. International awards include Prix Italia in radio programme series 1988, Goldene Nica prize at Ars Electronica festival, Linz, Austria, 1989.

Sallinen, Aulis (1935),
composer. Manager of the Radio Symphony Orchestra 1960–70, teacher at the Sibelius Academy 1965–76, artist professor since 1976. Sallinen's style has a polymorphic and original expression. He has composed symphonies, a cello concerto and music for children's choirs. His *The Horseman*, *The Red Line* and *The King Goes Forth to France* played a vital role in the rebirth of Finnish opera.

Salminen, Matti (1945)
opera bass singer. Soloist with the Finnish National Opera 1969–71, first bass with the Cologne Opera 1972–80, regular visiting singer with the Zürich Opera 1974–84, soloist since 1984. Regular visiting singer with Berlin Deutsche Oper, Bavarian and Hamburg operas, Vienna State Opera and Metropolitan Opera. Continuous visits to music centres throughout the world. Numerous recordings.

Salonen, Esa-Pekka (1958),
conductor, composer. Studied composition and conducting in both Finland and Italy. Chief conductor of the Swedish Radio Symphony Orchestra since 1987, visiting conductor of the London Philharmonic Orchestra 1985–88, regular visits to Oslo, also to Los Angeles where he has been chief conductor since 1992. Artistic Director of the Helsinki Festval 1995–96.

Saraste, Jukka (1956),
conductor. Visiting conductor with several orchestras in Finland and abroad, including Finnish Radio Symphony Orchestra 1985–87. Chief conductor of Scottish Chamber Orchestra since 1986. Chief conductor of Radio Symphony Orchestra since 1987. Conductor of Toronto Symphony Orchestra since 1994.

Sarpaneva, Timo (1926),
artistic director, professor. Graduated from School of Applied Arts 1948. Worked as designer and artistic director in several companies. Designed art glass and objects in glass, porcelain, steel and cast iron, as well as clothes. Numerous exhibitions in Finland and abroad, works in many museums. Among important international awards are the Lunning Prize and the Italian president's gold medal. Honorary doctorate from Royal College of Arts.

Saxén, Lauri (1927)
chancellor of the University of Helsinki. Doctor of Medicine and Surgery, Lic. Phil. Professor of experimental pathology 1967-93, chairman of the board of directors of the Institute of Biotechnology 1989-93, chancellor 1993-96. Member and chairman of several medical and cultural organisations. Numerous publications and lectures at home and abroad.

Sundberg, Matti (1942)
CEO, M. Sc. (Econ.). Occupied several positions of responsibility in industry, among them managing director of Metsä-Botnia 1976-86 and Ovako 1986-91. Since 1991 CEO of Valmet, a major Finnish high-tech multinational specialising in machine engineering.

Toikka, Oiva (1931),
industrial designer. Teacher at the School of Applied Arts 1960–63, designer at Arabia factory and Nuutajärvi Glass. Glass works include utility designs, art and unique pieces, as well as sculptures. He has exhibited abroad and has works displayed in many foreign museums. Awards include the coveted Lunning Prize 1970, Asahi Shimbun and Hokkaido Museum of Modern Art World Glass Now prize 1985.

Uosukainen, Riitta (1942)
speaker of the Finnish Parliament. M.A. (Phil.). Worked in publishing and as a Finnish language teacher in schools and universities. Member of Parliament since 1983. Minister of Education 1991–94, speaker of the Finnish Parliament since 1994. On the boards of several cultural organisations and companies. Author of a Finnish grammar.

Vainio, Vesa (1942)
CEO, Master of Laws. Occupied executive positions in many companies, most recently deputy managing director of the wood and paper company Kymmene Oy 1985–91 and its managing director 1991–92. Member of the board of many Finnish companies. Managing director of the Union Bank of Finland 1992–93 and its CEO 1993–95. CEO and chairman of the board of Merita Bank 1996–.

Uotinen, Jorma (1950)
internationally recognised ballet dancer and choreographer. Dancer with Finnish National Opera 1970–76, member of Group de Recherches Théâtrales de l´Opera de Paris. Dancing master with City of Helsinki Theatre 1982–91, member of the board and director of the dance group 1987–91. Director Finnish National Ballet since 1992. Choreographs include Trio, The Endless Enigma, The Forgotten Horizon, Unisono, Pierrot Lunaire, Kalevala, Ballet Pathetique, The Dance Floor on the Mountain and Cable, often in collaboration with Pirjo and Matti Bergström or Carolyn Carson. Choreography for the Finnish versions of the musicals Chicago and Cats.

Vänskä, Osmo (1953)
conductor, clarinetist. First place in the Besançon conductors competition 1982. Artistic director Crusell Week 1988–93, visiting conductor Lahti City Orchestra 1985–93, artistic director 1988–, artistic director Tapiola Sinfonietta 1990–92, artistic director Islandic Symphony Orchestra 1993–96, chief conductor BBC Scottish Symphony Orchestra since 1996. Numerous recordings with Lahti Orchestra, Tapiola Sinfonietta, Stockholm and Oslo philharmonic orchestras, Malmö and Sjaelland symphony orchestras, and Lahti Chamber Music Society. His Sibelius recordings have been particularly well received. Gramophone magazine and Grand Prix du Disque prizes.

Vikström, John (1931),
archbishop of the Evangelical Lutheran Church of Finland, Doctor of Theology. Teacher and reader at Åbo Academy in 1960s, assistant professor 1970. Occupied many administrative positions in the church in the 1970s, bishop of the diocese of Porvoo 1970–82, archbishop since 1982. Member of the central committee of the World Council of Churches since 1983. Published numerous works on religious subjects.

von Wright, Georg Henrik (1916)
professor, member of the Academy of Finland. Professor of philosophy or visiting professor at the universities of Helsinki, Cambridge, Cornell, California, Pittsburg, Karlsruhe and St. Andrews. Popular lecturer at home and abroad. Numerous publications of which the latest are Minervan pöllö, Myten om framsteget and The Tree of Knowledge. Honorary doctorates from the universities of Helsinki, Turku, Tampere, Stockholm, Lund, Tromsö, Liverpool, Bologna, Buenos Aires and Salta. Wihuri international prize 1976, Swedish Cultural Foundation prize 1982, Alexander von Humbolt Foundation prize 1986, Swedish Academy main prize 1986, Tollander prize 1987, Selma Lagerlöf literature prize 1993, and Logonomit's Speaker of the Year prize 1994.

SELECTED BIBLIOGRAPHY

General Works

Facts about Finland, Otava, 1996.
Find out about Finland, Otava, 1996.
Finland Handbook 1996, Comma Finland Oy and the Finnish Tourist Board, 1996
Focus on Finland, Otava, 1995.

Geography and Travels

Hautala, Hannu, A Summer's Night, Otava 1992.
Hautala, Hannu, Wild Water, Otava, 1994.
Hautala, Hannu, Winter in the Finnish Taiga, Helsinki, Otava, 1990.
Hautala, Hannu & Rautiainen, Lassi, Exploring Finland's National Parks, Otava, 1995.
Huovinen, Veikko & Hautala, Hannu, The Tale of Forest Folk, Otava, 1994.
Mäkelä, Eero, Finnish Cuisine à la Eero Mäkelä, 1992.
Mäkelä, Eero & Hottinger, Gero & Immonen, Pekka, New Flavours from Finland, Otava, 1995.
Niiniluoto, Maaret & Sandberg, Peter, Picture Finland, 1992.
Piri, Markku & Aalto, Jussi, Helsinki – Light and Shade, Otava, 1994.
Tanttu, Anna-Maija & Tanttu, Juha, Food from Finland, Otava, 1995.
Valta, Matti, Among the Islands, Otava, 1992.
Welin, P.-O. & Othman, Hans, Turku. Åbo. The City of Turku, Otava, 1990.

History and Politics

Alapuro, Risto, State and Revolution in Finland, The University of California Press, 1990.
Jutikkala, Eino & Pirinen, Kauko, A History of Finland, WSOY, 1996.
Kivikari, Urpo, The Legacy of Hansa, Otava, 1996.
Klinge, Matti, The Baltic World, 1995.
Klinge, Matti, Brief History of Finland, Otava, 1994.
Klinge, Matti, Let Us Be Finns, Otava 1992.
Mare Balticum, John Nurminen Foundation and Otava, 1995.
Zetterberg, Seppo, Finland after 1917, Otava, 1991.

Finnish Language and Dictionaries

Aaltio, Maija-Hellikki, Finnish for Foreigners, Otava, 1996.
CD-ROM Dictionary Finnish-English-Finnish (PC/Windows), WSOY, 1996
Hurme, Raija & Pesonen, Maritta & Syväoja, Olli, English-Finnish General Dictionary, WSOY, 1990.
Hurme, Raija & Malin & Syväoja, Olli, Finnish-English General Dictionary, WSOY, 1988.
Hurme, Raija & Malin & Syväoja, Olli, Finnish-English Concise Dictionary, WSOY, 1987.
Hurme, Raija & Malin & Syväoja, Olli, English-Finnish Student Dictionary, WSOY, 1994.
Joutsen, Dictionary of Legal Terms, WSOY, 1995.
Sovijärvi, Pocket Dictionary Finnish-English-Finnish, WSOY, 1995.

Art and Architecture

Ateneum Guide. From Wacklin to Wäinö Aaltonen. The Fine Arts Academy of Finland & Otava, 1987.
Bonk Business Inc., Otava, 1993.
Design by Marja Kurki. Text: Pekka Suhonen, photographs: Kaj G. Lindholm. Otava, 1996.
Hausen, Marika & Mikkola, Kirmo & Amberg, Anna-Liisa & Valto, Tytti, Eliel Saarinen. Projects 1886–1923. Otava, 1990.
Hausen, Marika, & Valto, Tytti, Hvitträsk. The Home as a Work of

Art, Otava, 1988.

Ilonen, Arvi, Helsinki; An Architectural Guide, Otava, 1990.

Linna – The Presidential Palace, Otava, 1992.

Minkkinen, Arno Rafael, Waterline, Otava, 1994.

Nikula, Riitta, Landscape and Architecture, Otava, 1993.

Ruoff, Eeva & Viljakainen, Timo, Gullranda – A Summer Home in Finland, WSOY, 1996.

Schildt, Göran, Alvar Aalto. A Life's work. Architecture, Design and Art, 1994.

Valkonen, Markku, Finnish Art over the Centuries, Otava, 1992.

Music and Literature

Ågren, Gösta, The Valley in the Midst of Violence, Bloodaxe, 1992.

Carpelan, Bo, Axel, Grafton Books, 1991.

Forsström, Tua, The Snow Leopard, Bloodaxe, 1990.

Haavikko, Paavo, Selected Poems, Carcanet, 1991.

Haavio, Martti, Väinämöinen: Eternal Sage, Suomalainen tiedeakatemia: Tiedekirja, 1991.

Huldén, Lars, The Chain Dance, Camden House, 1991.

Idström, Annika, My Brother Sebastian, Forest Books, 1992

Jansson, Tove, Comet in Moominland, Farrar, Straus & Giroux, 1992.

Joenpelto, Eeva, The Bride of Life, FATA, 1995.

The Kalevala. Epic of the Finnish People, Otava, 1988.

Kihlman, Christer, The Blue Mother, University of Nebraska Press, 1990.

Kivi, Aleksis, Seven Brothers, Finnish-American Translators' Association, 1991.

Kurtén, Björn, The innocent Assassins: Biological Eaasys on Life in the Present and Distant Past, Columbia University Press, 1991.

Lampi, Heimo, Death Stalks Meteora, Vantage Press, 1995.

Lander, Leena, Cast a Long Shadow, Second Story Press, 1995.

Lehtinen, Lasse, Blood, Sweat and Bears, Brasseys, 1990.

Linna, Väinö, The Unknown Soldier, WSOY, 1982.

Meri, Veijo, Private Jokinen's Marriage Leave, Nemzetközi szinházi intézet, 1990.

Paasilinna, Arto, The Year of the Hare, Peter Owen, 1995.

Päätalo, Kalle, Our Daily Bread, Finn Heritage, 1990.

Parland, Oscar, The Year of the Bull, Peter Owen, 1991.

Saaritsa, Pentti, Gathering Fragments, Penumbra Press, 1991.

Sillanpää, F.E., The Maid Silja, Cherokee, 1990.

Simonsuuri, Kirsti, Boy Devil, Exile, 1992.

Södergran, Edith, Complete Poems, Bloodaxe, 1992.

Stenberg, Eira, Wings of Hope and Daring: Selected Poems, Bloodaxe, 1992.

Turkka, Sirkka, Not You. Not the Rain. University of Nebraska Press, 1991.

Utrio, Kaari, The Spring of the Moonstone, Kalevala Koru and Otava, 1995.

Waltari, Mika, The Dark Angel or Johannes Angelos, WSOY, 1989.

Valkonen, Kaija and Markku, Festival Fever, Otava 1994.

Valtonen, Mato & Järvenpää, Sakke & Hämäläinen, Seppo, Merry Christmas Leningrad Cowboys, 1994.

Illustrations:
Defence forces archives p. 176, 179; Disabled War Veterans' Association of Finland p. 87; El Rod Oy Opa p. 136; Finland's Soprtmuseum Foundation p. 159; Finnair p. 183; Oy Fiskars Ab p. 75; Fotoni p. 23; Hannu Hautala p. 9 (below); Helo Oy p. 171; Helsinki University of Technology p. 108; Harri Hietala p. 102; Seppo Hilpo p. 147 (below); Urpo Häyrinen pp. 21, 30, 33; Iittala-Nuutajärvi Oy p. 134 (below); Tove Jansson p. 123; Juha Kalliolahti p. 13; Seppo Keränen p. 10 (above); Juhani Kohonen p. 115; Kone oy p. 175; Kværner Masa-Yards 69 Lehtikuva pp. 36–37, 54, 58, 65 (above), 81, 96–97, 107, 124–125, 129, 130–131, 133, 140 (above), 160–161, 162 (both), 168–169, Leipätiedotus p. 164; Pekka Lempiäinen p. 22, 99, 104, 166–167; Anneke Lipsanen p. 114; Luonnonkuva-arkisto p.89; Luhta Oy p. 77; Museum of Finnish Architecture pp. 140–141 (below), 145; Museum of Finnish Industrial Design pp. 116, 134; Lauri Mäkinen pp. 4, 12, 52, 83, 100; Juha Mälkönen p. 9 (above); Oy Nautor Ab p. 70–71; Oy Nokia Ab pp. 75, Paavo Ojasti p. 5; Otava pp. 46, 53; Pressfoto pp. 18 (below), 48, 64–65, 80, 105; Martti Rantanen p. 72 (above); Rautakirja Oy pp. 154–155; Arno Rautavaara pp. 10–11 (below); Tapani Romppainen p. 95; Matti Ruotsalainen pp. 31, 46, 50, 127, 128, 146; Ritva Räty p. 170; P. Sarvas p. 42; Sky-Foto pp. 7 (both), 92–93; Studio Pitkänen Ky p. 40; Heikki Suni p. 62; Suomen selkäinsti-tuutti p. 85; Vaisala Oy p. 74; Valio p. 24 (both); Valmet Oy p. 71; Matti Valta pp. 16–17; Rafael Wardi p. 147 (above); P.-O. Welin pp. 26–27, 28, 29, 35, 44–45; Viking Line p. 18 (above); Yhtyneet Kuvalehdet pp. 14–15, 56, 60–61, 138–139, 143, 148–149, 151, 153, Yhtyneet paperitehtaat p. 72–73.